19 世纪的外滩，大上海由这里起步

The Bund in the 19th century—Shanghai Stemming From Here

美好城市的百年变迁

——明信片上看上海

The Centennial Changes of the Dynamic City

Seeing Shanghai From the Postcards

【上册】 Vol. I

姚丽旋　编著

Compiled by Yao Lixuan

上海大学出版社

Shanghai University Press

前言

明信片的问世，距今已有140年的历史。1869年奥地利发行了世界上第一张明信片，从此明信片成为一种简便的邮政函件。中国早期的明信片多为外商书信馆发行，直到1897年，清政府邮政正式发行了中国的第一张明信片。明信片分邮资片和无邮资片两大类，又有邮政部门和非邮政部门发行之分，其形式与用途多种多样。1893年瑞士首发印有图像的美术明信片，后来又派生出图画明信片和摄影明信片。摄影术与印刷术的结合，使明信片的内容愈加丰富多彩，尤其是反映各国城市风光的明信片，流行广泛，风靡全球。

19世纪末，上海滩开始出现城市风光明信片。一张张明信片，就是一页页历史，记载着上海城市建设的过去和现在。一百多年来，上海开埠通商、社会变革、几经战乱以及不断改造更新的城区建设所体现出的开放性、流通性、周期性、持续性，也同时表现在明信片的发行上。上海明信片成为这座城市发展的见证，随其兴衰，与其同行。当把这些从国内外收集到的明信片，按时空有序地排列在一起，或者从一个视角去审视各处建筑的新旧变化，感慨城市的沧桑巨变，百年似是转瞬之间……

时光的印痕，历史的缩影，一幅图片有时胜过千言万语。明信片史料真实客观，内容丰富，特别是20世纪前叶的老明信片，为不可多得的第一手影像资料。这些影像资料有的被本届世博会上海馆选用。同时，本书又被上海市新闻出版局列为“上海世博图书出版工程”项目，并评选为上海世博会特许产品。在此特别感谢上海市新闻出版局对本书发行给予的支持。也十分感谢上海大学出版社的责任编辑傅玉芳、柯国富为此书出版所作的精心策划与设计。在本书素材收集、整理编排、英文翻译及编写的过程中，曾得到陆宁榕、赵智楠、傅敏、吴荻、姚青予、沈洪、孟庆杰、于吉星等多方的帮助，一并表示衷心的感谢！

由于上海风光明信片其内容取材大多集中在主要街区和著名景观，反映城市全貌存在着局限性。另外本人对上海历史的研究及知识有限，书中难免存在不足和错误之处，恳请读者批评指正。

姚丽旋

2010年3月

Preface

One hundred and forty years have passed since the first postcard came out. In 1869, the first postcard in the world was issued in Austria and thence postcard became a handy postal letter. Most of the early postcards in China were issued by foreign post office. Not until 1897, the post office of Qing Government issued China's first postcard. Postcards are divided into two types, postcards with postage and postcards without postage. Some are issued by the post office and some are not with various forms and purposes. In 1893 Switzerland issued a picture card with image printed on it and later pictorial postcard and photography postcard came into being. The combination of photography and printing makes postcards more colorful. Especially the postcards that reflect the cityscape of various countries are very prevalent.

In the late 19th century, postcards describing the cityscape came into being in Shanghai. A postcard is a sheet of history recording the past and present of Shanghai's city construction. The openness, negotiability, periodicity and continuity which were reflected by Shanghai's opening as a commercial port, the social changes, chaos caused by war and transformation and innovation of the city construction during more than 100 years can also be showed on the issue of the postcards. The postcards of Shanghai become the witness of its development. When we sorted out the postcards collected from home and abroad on the city landscape of Shanghai sorted out according to temporal and spatial variation, or survey the changes of the specific construction from one perspective, we exclaim over the dramatic changes of this city. It seems that one hundred years just pass away in a twinkle···

The steps of time, the epitome of history and the dramatic changes of the city rise before our eyes. Picture says a thousand words. Postcards are objective historical material. Especially the old postcards in the first half of the 20th century are precious firsthand picture materials. Some of these picture materials have been used by Shanghai Pavilion of the Expo. Meanwhile, this book has been listed by Shanghai Press and Publication Administration as one item in the Shanghai Expo Book Publishing Project and regarded as a licensed product. I'd like to offer my sincere thanks to a host of people who have done a lot for this book. Firstly, I'd like to offer my thanks to Shanghai Press and Publication Administration, for their support to the issue of this book. Secondly, to Fu Yufang, Ke Guofu, editors in charge of Shanghai University Press for their well design. Thirdly, to Lu Ningrong, Zhao Zhinan, Fu Min, Wu Di, Yao Qingyu, Shen Hong, Meng Qingjie, Yu Jixing, who have done so much in the material gathering, arranging, compiling and translating work.

Because the contents of the postcards on the cityscape of Shanghai mainly focus on the main blocks and famous landscape, there is the limitation for them to reflect the full view of the city. Additionally, due to the author's limited knowledge and research on the history of Shanghai, there must be remaining errors and rooms for improvement for which your valuable comments, suggestions and criticisms are welcomed.

Yao Lixuan

March, 2010

目录
Contents

【上册】
Vol.I

【下 册】Vol.II

POST CARD.
REICHSPOST
SHANGHAI
POST
大清朱家角郵局
中華人民共和國
開國一週年紀念
800圓
1949
1950
中國人民郵政
1950-10-1
上海
UNION POSTALE
22 MAR 15
POST

一

老　城　厢

Shanghai Old Town

老城厢即上海县城城墙内外约7平方公里区域的统称，是上海这座名城的发祥地。上海县于元代（1291年）建立，当时仅有人口6万多户。为了防止倭寇侵袭，1553年建造城墙；为了繁荣和经济发展，1912年拆城筑路。如今由中华路与人民路衔接而成的环形路，就是过去城壕的地基。七百年的风雨沧桑，一百年的历史巨变，老城厢仍传承着这座城市的历史文脉，因为这里留有上海的老地方，保存着人们的老记忆。

Shanghai Old Town, the cradleland of Shanghai, refers to the seven square kilometers' area from the inner part to the outer part of the city wall of Shanghai County. Shanghai County was established in Yuan Dynasty (1291) with only about 60 thousand families at that time. To guard against the Japanese invaders, the city wall was built in 1553. For prosperity and the development of economy, the wall was removed and roads were paved in 1912. Now the circular road formed by the junction of Zhonghua Road and Renmin Road was the previous base of the moat. Through 700 years of social vicissitudes and 100 years of drastic changes, the Old Town still passes on the city's historical essence because with many old places of Shanghai, it holds people's old memories.

一 老城厢 Shanghai Old Town

1898 年中国编制的上海地图

Map of Shanghai made in China in 1898

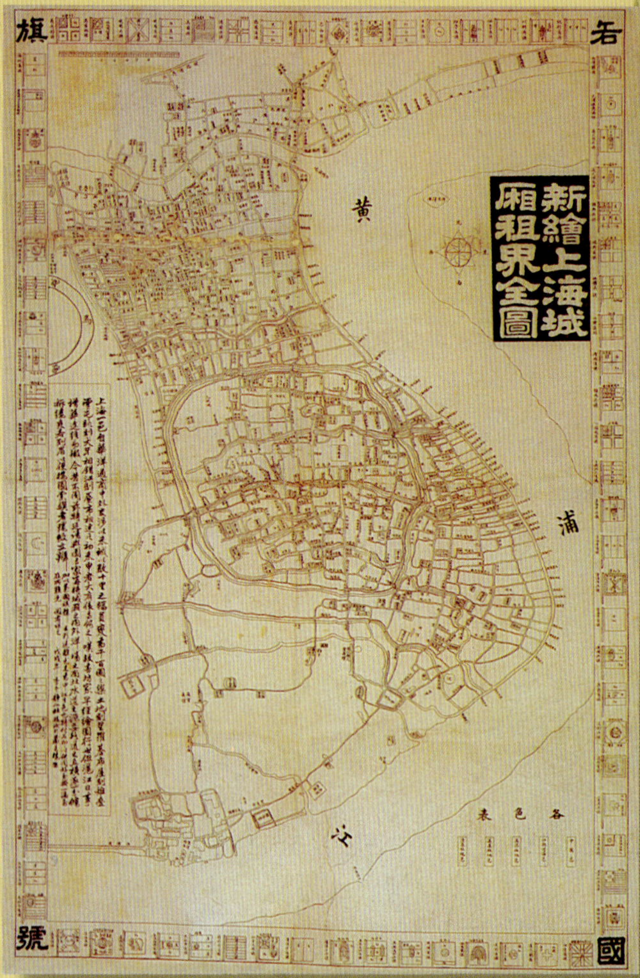

清末老城墙

The ancient citywall in the late Qing Dynasty

20 世纪初护城河几尽干涸

The moat almost dried up in the 1900s

干涸的护城河

The moat almost dried up

一
老城厢 Shanghai Old Town

连接老城厢与法租界的桥

Bridge between the Old Town and the French Concession

1898 年建于法租界的水塔

Water tower built in the French concession in 1898

- 重建于 1815 年的大境阁
- Dajing Pavilion rebuilt in 1815

- 上海仅存的明代古城墙遗址
- The only existing site of the ancient city of Ming Dynasty in Shanghai

一 老城厢 Shanghai Old Town

流入宝带门（小东门）的方浜河

Fangbang River flows into Baodai Gate (Minor East Gate)

城外的河浜与木桥

River and wood bridge outside the city

● 老城晏海门（老北门）

● Yanhai Gate of the Old City (The Old North Gate)

● 老城晏海门（老北门）

● Yanhai Gate of the Old City (The Old North Gate)

一 老城厢 Shanghai Old Town

大清朱家角郵局

建于1860年的障川门（新北门）外景，今丽水路北端

The outside scene of Zhangchuan Gate (The New North Gate) built in 1860. (Today's north end of Lishui Road)

新北门外城河浜

Creek outside the New North Gate

老城外街景

The street scene outside the old city

早期的雷允上药店

The early Leiyunshang pharmacy

一 老城厢 Shanghai Old Town

设在城门边的彩票行

Lottery office at the side of the city gate

老城出入口及待客的人力车

The gateway of the ancient city and the rickshaws a waiting passengers

老城入口

The entrance to the old city

老城入口

The entrance to the old city

一 老城厢 Shanghai Old Town

● 城门及瓮城

● The city gate and the barbican entrance to the city

● 城内殿台楼阁

● Palaces and pavilions in the city

一 老城厢 Shanghai Old Town

- 建于1836年的“大千胜境”石牌坊
- Daqianshengjing Stone archway built in 1836

- 城内居民
- Residents in the city

● 始建于南宋时期的文庙，也称孔庙，历史上几经修建

● Wen Miao also called the Confucius Temple was first built in South Song Dynasty and reconstructed for many times in history

● 1980 年修建后的文庙

● Wen Miao rebuilt in 1980

一 老城厢 Shanghai Old Town

20 世纪初的城隍庙

Town God's Temple in the 1900s

21 世纪初的城隍庙

Town God's Temple in the 2000s

城隍庙成为上海最热闹的地方

Town God's Temple becomes the busiest place in Shanghai

热闹的城隍庙

The hustle and bustle in Town God's Temple

一 老城厢 Shanghai Old Town

● 豫园始建于1559年，是上海最早的私家花园

● Yu Garden, first built in 1559, was the earliest private garden in Shanghai

● 豫园旧景

● The old scene of Yu Garden

豫园旧景

The old scene of Yu Garden

豫园一景

A scene of Yu Garden

● 建于明代保存至今的豫园大假山

● The artificial hillock in Yu Garden built in Ming Dynasty is still kept intact now

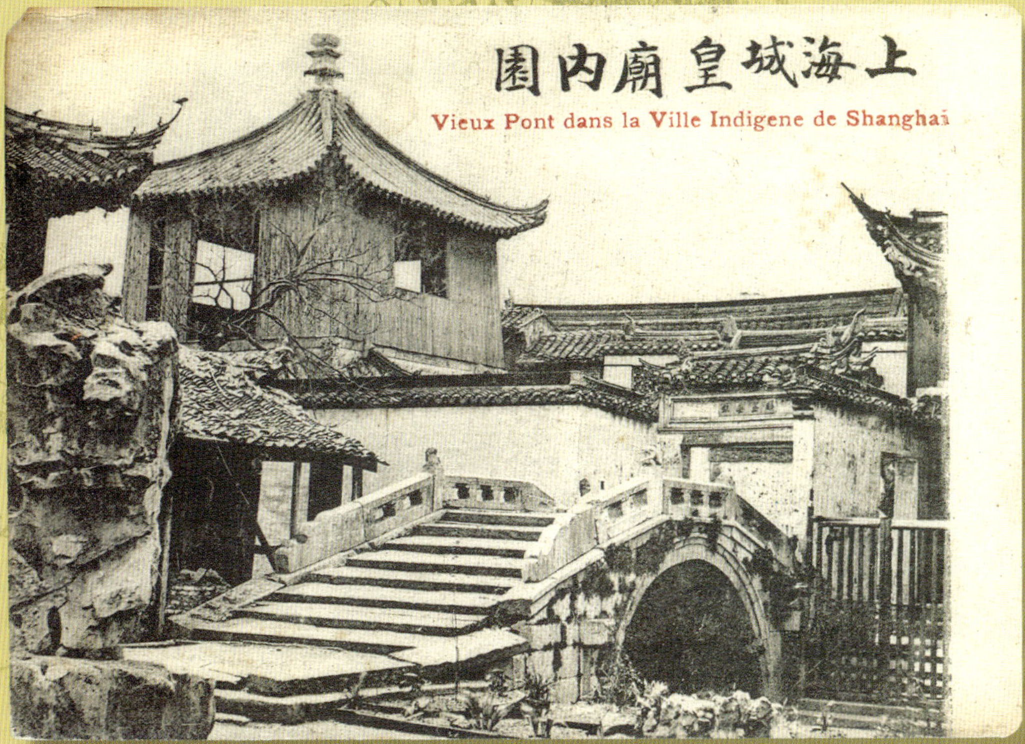

● 城隍庙内园
● The inner garden of Town God's Temple

● 内园建于1776年，1956年归入豫园
● Inner garden built in 1776 was merged into Yu Garden in 1956

一 老城厢 Shanghai Old Town

● 建于1784年的豫园湖心亭茶楼

● The teahouse in the pavilion at the center of the lake in Yu Garden built in 1784

● 20世纪初的湖心亭和九曲桥

● The pavilion at the center of the lake and the zigzag bridge in the 1900s

1926年九曲桥改建为水泥桥

The zigzag bridge was made into a concrete bridge in 1926

湖心亭和九曲桥

The pavilion at the center of the lake and the zigzag bridge

一 老城厢 Shanghai Old Town

● 20世纪50年代的湖心亭，荷花池中保留有李平书塑像，其在清末时主持了上海的一系列社会改良活动

● The pavilion at the center of the lake in the 1950s. There's a statue of Li Pingshu in the lotus pond who has hosted a series of social reform activities in Shanghai in the late Qing Dynasty

● 20世纪70年代的湖心亭和九曲桥

● The pavilion at the center of the lake and the zigzag bridge in the 1970s

20 世纪 90 年代的湖心亭和九曲桥

The pavilion at the center of the lake and the zigzag bridge in the 1990s

21 世纪初的湖心亭和九曲桥

The pavilion at the center of the lake and the zigzag bridge in the 2000s

一 老城厢 Shanghai Old Town

● 城墙下的街市

● Downtown streets by the city wall

● 城墙下的街市

● Downtown streets by the city wall

● 清末城内街市

● The street and market in the city in the late Qing Dynasty

● 清末城内街市

● The street and market in the city in the late Qing Dynasty

一 老城厢 Shanghai Old Town

大兴恒号布店

Daxingheng cloth store

瓷器街店

Porcelain store

● 清末的宝华照相馆

● Baohua photo studio in the late Qing Dynasty

● 民国初的宝华照相馆

● Baohua photo studio in the early period of the Republic of China

● 酱园

● Sauce and pickles shop

● 当铺

● Pawnshop

小贩营生

Peddlers were earning their living

小贩营生

Peddlers were earning their living

一 老城厢 Shanghai Old Town

- 沿街的地摊和棚店
- Stalls and stores along the street

● 弄堂里的店铺

● Stores in the lane

● 弄堂里的店铺

● Stores in the lane

一 老城厢 Shanghai Old Town

创办于1910年的松月楼素菜馆

Songyuelou vegetarian restaurant opened in 1910

沿街的馄饨店

Wonton restaurant in the street

● 方浜路上的茶馆与饭店

● Teahouse and hotel on Fangbang Road

流动的小食担

Roving Chow stalls

街头排挡

Sidewalk snack booths in the street

● 百姓生计

● Livelihood of ordinary people

● 百姓生计

● Livelihood of ordinary people

一 老城厢 Shanghai Old Town

城内民居

Residences in the city

城内石桥

The stone bridge in the city

- 城内民居
- Residences in the city

- 城内民居
- Residences in the city

热闹的市井

Crowded and busy marketplace

热闹的市井

Crowded and busy marketplace

街头表演

Street Performance

街头表演

Street Performance

一 老城厢 Shanghai Old Town

城边的剃头摊

The barber's by the citywall

街边的梳理店

Chinese Women's Barber at the roadside

- 1912 年拆城填壕筑民国路，今为人民路
- Minguo Road built in 1912 (today's Renmin Road)

● 1913年在上海县署设立的警察所，位于今蓬莱路

● The police station was set up in Shanghai County in 1913 and it is located on today's Penglai Road

● 20世纪30年代的小东门

● Minor East Gate in the 1930s

● 20 世纪 30 年代的城厢街景

● The street scene of the Old Town in the 1930s

● 20 世纪 30 年代的城厢街景

● The street scene of the Old Town in the 1930s

老城学堂

The school of the Old Town

露天学堂

The school in the open air

千变万化的西洋镜

The ever-changing zoetrope

街边书摊

Bookstall in the street

一 老城厢 Shanghai Old Town

大清朱家角郵局

流动演出

Roving performance

大众戏棚

Popular matshed theatre

豫园古戏台

The old stage in Yu Garden

茶楼音乐会

Concert in the teahouse

20世纪70年代的弄堂旧影

The old scene of the lane in the 1970s

弄堂里的生活

People's lives in the lane

老城厢里的大境路

Dajing Road in the Old Town

保持原貌的安仁街

Unchanged Anren Street

一 老城厢 Shanghai Old Town

弄堂里的生活

People's lives in the lane

建于1763年的"书隐楼"遗址

Ruins of Shuying Pavilion built in 1763

老城厢三山会馆

San Shan Community in the old town

变化中的老城厢

The changing old town

变化中的老城厢

The changing old town

1999 年方浜中路建成上海老街

Middle Fangbang Road was built into Shanghai Old Street in 1999

上海老街远眺

An old view of Shanghai Old Street

一

老城厢 Shanghai Old Town

东台路古玩市场

Antique market on Dongtai Road

豫园雪景

Snowscape in Yu Garden

豫园新貌

A new look of Yu Garden

豫园新貌

A new look of Yu Garden

一

老城厢 Shanghai Old Town

豫园商城

Yuyuan Store

豫园商城

Yuyuan Store

凝晖阁与华宝楼

Ninghui Pavilion and Huabao Pavilion

城隍庙畅煦楼

Changxu Pavilion in the Town God's Temple

21 世纪初的湖心亭与九曲桥鸟瞰

A bird's eye view of the lake-center pavilion and the zigzag bridge in the 2000s

21 世纪初的老城厢

The old town in the 2000s

二

黄 浦 江

Huangpu River

黄浦江发源于淀山湖，至吴淞口出海，全长113.4公里。历史上黄浦江曾是吴淞江的支流，明代永乐年间（1403—1424年）“淞浦合流”水利工程使之与长江和东海相连，成为流经上海的最大河流。黄浦江以其优越的自然条件和历史机缘孕育了漕运枢纽和上海港的发展。一百多年来，浦江两岸的演变正是中国从屈辱走向解放与现代化的写照。人民依托黄浦江造就了国际大都市的繁荣，黄浦江被誉为上海的母亲河。

Huangpu River takes its rise from Dianshan Lake and goes to the sea at Wusongkou with a length of 113.4 kilometers. In history, Huangpu River was a tributary of Wusong River. During the Yongle period in Ming Dynasty(1403-1424), the water conservancy project called “the combination of Wusong River and Huangpu River” made it link with Yangtze River and East China Sea, thus becoming the largest river passing Shanghai. By its favorable natural condition and historical conjuncture, Huangpu River nurtures the development of canal transportation and the Port of Shanghai. During more than 100 years, the development of the two sides of the Huangpu River is exactly the epitome of China's development from humiliation to liberation and modernization. Huangpu River is praised as the mother river of Shanghai. Relying on this river, people have created the prosperity of this cosmopolitan city.

二

黄浦江 Huangpu River

20世纪初的浦江两岸

The two sides of Huangpu River in the 1900s

20世纪初的浦江两岸

The two sides of Huangpu River in the 1900s

引水灌田

Irrigating the fields

浦江夜渡

Crossing Huangpu River in the night

二

黄浦江 Huangpu River

大清朱家角邮局

- 江边船坞
- Boatyard along the river

江边木号

The commercial household along the river

江边木号

The commercial household along the river

二 黄浦江 Huangpu River

- 吴淞口因是吴淞江的出海口而得名
- Wusongkou gets its name becawe it is the outlet to Wusong River

吴淞口的船只

Vessels at Wusongkou

吴淞口的信号台

Signal station at Wusongkou

● 始建于1660年的吴淞炮台

● Wusong emplacement built in 1660

● 1932年的吴淞炮台

● Wusong emplacement in 1932

20世纪初的吴淞镇

Wusong Town in the 1900s

20世纪30年代的吴淞镇

Wusong Town in the 1930s

二
黄浦江
Huangpu River

● 吴淞口水位测量装置
● Level measuring device of Wusongkou

● 吴淞口的灯塔
● Lighthouse of Wusongkou

20 世纪 80 年代的吴淞口

Wusongkou in the 1980s

20 世纪 80 年代的吴淞口

Wusongkou in the 1980s

二 黄浦江 Huangpu River

大清朱家角郵局

由外滩花园看黄浦江

Viewing Huangpu River from Bund Garden

黄浦江旧景

An old scene of Huangpu River

● 过江摆渡

● Sampans for going across the river

● 过江摆渡

● Sampans for going across the river

二 黄浦江 Huangpu River

大清朱家角郵局

浦江上的民船

Civilian craft on Huangpu River

浦江上的清军战船

Warships of the army of the Qing Dynasty on Huangpu River

浦江上的鸦片囤船

Opium godowns on Huangpu River

浦江上的鸦片囤船

Opium godowns on Huangpu River

二
黄浦江 Huangpu River

浦江上的外国军舰

Foreign warships on Huangpu River

浦江上的外国军舰

Foreign warships on Huangpu River

● 游弋于浦江的列强炮舰

● Gunboats of the big powers cruising on Huangpu River

● 游弋于浦江的列强炮舰

● Gunboats of the big powers cruising on Huangpu River

二
黄浦江
Huangpu River

沿江码头

Wharf along the river

沿江码头

Wharf along the river

● 20 世纪初进港的客货轮船

● The cargos and passenger liners came in to the harbor in the 1900s

● 20 世纪 30 年代进港的客货轮船

● The cargos and passenger liners came in to the harbor in the 1930s

二 黄浦江 Huangpu River

● 20 世纪 20 年代浦江景象

● The scenery of Huangpu River in the 1920s

● 船上的庆典活动

● The celebration activities held on the boats

- 20世纪30年代浦江景象
- The scenery of Huangpu River in the 1930s

- 繁忙的运输船队
- The busy transport ships

20世纪50年代建设中的码头

The wharf being built in the 1950s

1971年12月21日“郑州”远洋货轮下水

The seagoing freighter called "Zheng Zhou" launched on December 21st, 1971

- 20世纪80年代的上海港
- Port of Shanghai in the 1980s

二 黄浦江 Huangpu River

清末时期的陆家嘴

Lujiazui in the late Qing Dynasty

清末时期的陆家嘴

Lujiazui in the late Qing Dynasty

● 陆家嘴江滩

● The beach of Huangpu River in Lujiazui

● 陆家嘴摆渡码头

● Wharf in Lujiazui for mooring wherries

20世纪初的陆家嘴

Lujiazui in the 1900s

20世纪初的陆家嘴

Lujiazui in the 1900s

20 世纪 20 年代由外滩看浦东

Seeing Pudong from the Bund in the 1920s

20 世纪 80 年代由外滩看浦东

Seeing Pudong from the Bund in the 1980s

二

黄浦江 Huangpu River

20世纪20年代由浦东看外滩

Seeing the Bund from Pudong in the 1920s

20世纪90年代由浦东看外滩

Seeing the Bund from Pudong in the 1990s

● 20 世纪 20 年代由浦东看外滩

● Seeing the Bund from Pudong in the 1920s

● 21 世纪初由浦东看外滩

● Seeing the Bund from Pudong in the 2000s

二
黄浦江 Huangpu River

20世纪30年代的陆家嘴

Lujiazui in the 1930s

20世纪80年代的陆家嘴

Lujiazui in the 1980s

20世纪90年代的陆家嘴

Lujiazui in the 1990s

20世纪90年代的陆家嘴

Lujiazui in the 1990s

- 1995年建成的东方明珠塔（468米）
- The Oriental Pearl TV Tower was built in 1995(468m)

二 黄浦江 Huangpu River

- 1999年建成的金茂大厦（420.5米）
- Jin Mao Tower was built in 1999(420.5m)

- 20世纪90年代的陆家嘴
- Lujiazui in the 1990s

- 20世纪90年代的陆家嘴
- Lujiazui in the 1990s

二 黄浦江 Huangpu River

陆家嘴晚霞

Twilight of Lujiazui

陆家嘴晚霞

Twilight of Lujiazui

● 耀眼的光环

● Halo-encircled Jin Mao Tower

● 大珠小珠落玉盘

● Big and small pearls dropping on the jade tray

二 黄浦江 Huangpu River

大清朱家角邮局

黄浦江F1摩托艇大赛

The F1 Motorboat Race on Huangpu River

陆家嘴鸟瞰

A bird's eye view of Lujiazui

陆家嘴夜色

The night of Lujiazui

陆家嘴夜色

The night of Lujiazui

二

黄浦江
Huangpu River

大清朱家角郵局

1865年成立的江南制造局于1867年迁至黄浦江边。为晚清最大的兵工厂，创造了中国兵器和造船史上多项第一

Jiangnan Manufacture Bureau built in 1865 moved to the bank of the Huangpu River in 1867. It was the largest ordnance factory of the late Qing Dynasty which created many firsts in China's history of weapon and shipbuilding

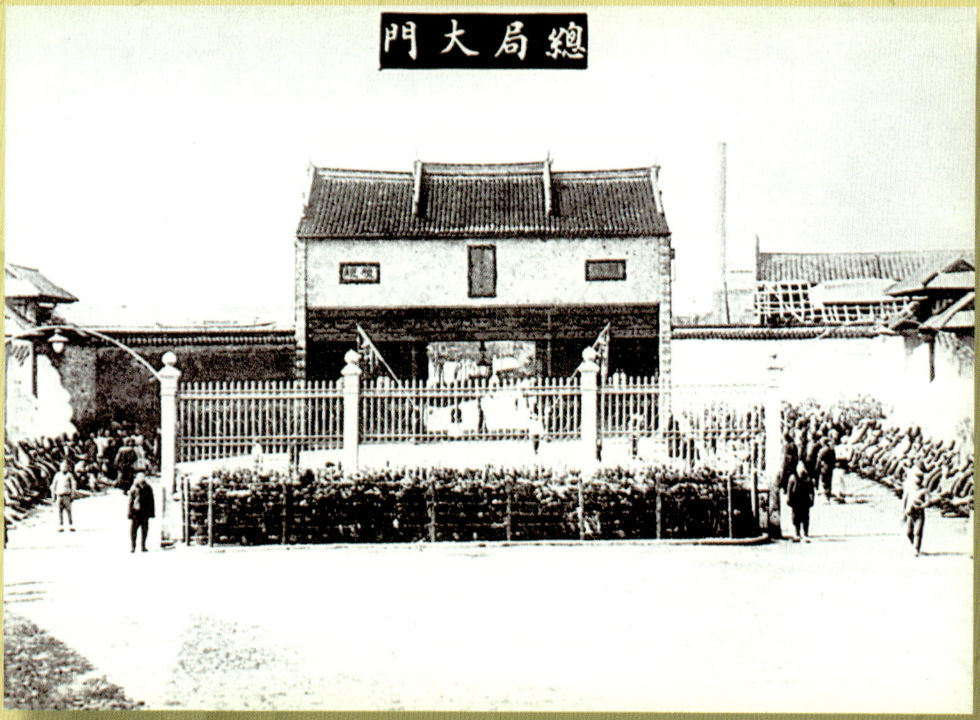

1911 年辛亥革命后改称上海制造局

The name was changed to Shanghai Manufacture Bureau after the revolution of 1911

1953 年改称江南造船厂，该址现为上海世博会园区

The name was changed to Jiangnan Shipyard in 1953, and now it is the site of the 2010 Shanghai World Expo

二

黄浦江 Huangpu River

大清朱家角邮局

● 半淞园于1909年建于黄浦江边。1920年5月8日毛泽东与新民学会会员在此聚会，欢送赴法勤工俭学人员。该园1937年毁于战火，园址在上海世博会园区浦西段

● Half Wusong Garden was built along the bank of Huangpu River in 1909. Mao Zedong and the members of Xinmin institute gathered there on May 8th, 1920 to see off the personnel who would work and study in Paris. It was destroyed in war in 1937 and the site of this garden was the Puxi part of the Shanghai World Expo site

● 半淞园风景

● The landscape of Half Wusong Garden

半淞园风景

The landscape of Half Wusong Garden

半淞园风景

The landscape of Half Wusong Garden

二 黄浦江 Huangpu River

● 2010年中国在上海举办以"城市，让生活更美好"为主题的世界博览会

● 2010 World Expo is held in Shanghai, China under the theme of "Better City, Better Life"

● 上海世博会园区位于南浦大桥西侧浦江两岸

● The Expo Site is located at the west side of Nanpu Bridge on both sides of Huangpu River

● 中国馆

● China Pavilion

● 世博轴

● Expo Axis

二
黄浦江 Huangpu River
大清朱家角邮局

● 2010年中国邮政发行中国馆等纪念邮票

● Commemorative stamps such as China Pavilion Stamps are issued by China Post in 2010

● 演艺中心于2010年2月更名为文化中心

● Performance Center was renamed as Culture Center in February, 2010

世博中心

Expo Center

主题馆

Theme Pavilion

二

黄浦江 Huangpu River

1976年建成的浦江第一桥——松浦大桥，至2010年黄浦江上建有10座大桥

The first bridge on Huangpu River—Songpu Bridge was built in 1976 and till 2010 there are 10 bridges built on Huangpu River

外滩观光隧道于2000年建成。1971年上海建成浦江第一条隧道——打浦路隧道，至2010年黄浦江已建在建隧道13条

The Bund Sight-seeing Tunnel was built in 2000. The first tunnel of Shanghai across Huangpu River—Da Pu Road tunnel was built in 1971 and till 2010 there are 13 tunnels built or being built across Huangpu River

1991 年建成的南浦大桥

Nanpu Bridge built in 1991

南浦大桥

Nanpu Bridge

二 黄浦江 Huangpu River

1993年建成的杨浦大桥

Yangpu Bridge built in 1993

杨浦大桥

Yangpu Bridge

1997 年建成的徐浦大桥

Xupu Bridge built in 1997

徐浦大桥

Xupu Bridge

2003年建成的卢浦大桥

Lupu Bridge built in 2003

建造中的卢浦大桥

Lupu Bridge under construction

● 黄浦江发源于淀山湖口淀峰

● Huangpu River rises in Koudian Mountain of Dian Shan Lake

● 黄浦江由吴淞口出海，与长江和东海交汇

● Huangpu River sets out from Wusongkou crossing Yangtze River and East China Sea

二 黄浦江 Huangpu River

20 世纪 40 年代的黄浦江

Huangpu River in the 1940s

复兴岛是黄浦江唯一的江心岛，1949 年 5 月蒋介石从复兴岛乘船逃往台湾

Fuxing Island is the only ait on Huangpu River. In May 1949, Chiang Kai-shek escaped to Taiwan by sea from Fuxing Island

20世纪80年代黄浦江上的行船

Ships on Huangpu River in the 1980s

20世纪80年代黄浦江上的行船

Ships on Huangpu River in the 1980s

二

黄浦江 Huangpu River

黄浦江晨曦

Dawning over the Huangpu River

黄浦江夕照

The Huangpu River at sunset

● 陆家嘴高处看浦江

● Seeing Huangpu River from a high place of Lujiazui

二 黄浦江 Huangpu River

浦江两岸风貌

The scenery on both sides of the Huangpu River

浦江两岸风貌

The scenery on both sides of the Huangpu River

浦江纵览

Panorama of Huangpu River

浦江纵览

Panorama of Huangpu River

二

黄浦江 Huangpu River

灯火璀璨的浦江夜景

The night view of Huangpu River

灯火璀璨的浦江夜景

The night view of Huangpu River

三

苏 州 河

Suzhou River

苏州河原是流经上海市吴淞江的下游河道，长53.4公里。1916年开挖疏浚后称为苏州河。苏州河的内河航运功能使其成为连接黄浦江与大运河的一条贸易通道，两岸聚集起各类工厂、仓储、文化、居住等建筑，堪称上海民族工业的摇篮。苏州河上曾有22个渡口，1856年建成第一座木桥，随后铁桥、水泥桥陆续诞生，现有桥梁30座。当年污染严重的苏州河，已成为今日城市的景观河以及未来的生态河。

Suzhou River with a length of 53.4 kilometers was originally a downstream channel passing Wusong River in Shanghai . After excavating and dredging, it was named Suzhou River in 1916. The function of river transportation made Suzhou River a trade route linking Huangpu River and the Grand Canal. With a gathering of architectures on both sides for industrial, storage, cultural and habitation purposes, it claims to be the cradle of Shanghai's national industry. There were once 22 ferries on Suzhou River and the first wooden bridge was built in 1856. Afterwards, iron bridges and concrete bridges came into being. Now there are altogether 30 bridges. The former Suzhou River with serious pollution has become today's scenery river and the future ecological river.

三

苏州河 Suzhou River

昔日苏州河

Suzhou River in former times

苏州河旧景

The old scene on Suzhou River

● 昔日苏州河与黄浦江交汇处

● The intersection of Suzhou River and Huangpu River in former times

● 英商建于1856年的威尔斯吊桥，中国人交费才能通过

● Wales Suspension Bridge was built by the British merchants in 1856. The Chinese cannot pass it unless paying first

三 苏州河 Suzhou River

● 1873年新建的木桥与外滩花园相邻，地处外摆渡口又不收费，故被称做公园桥或外白渡桥

● Adjacent to Bund Garden the newly built wooden bridge in 1873 was located on a ferry point, People can pass it without paying any fee, so it was called Garden Bridge or Waibaidu Bridge toll—fyee bridge

● 1882 年上海的第一盏电灯

● The first electric light of Shanghai in 1882

- 20世纪初的外白渡桥
- Waibaidu Bridge in the 1900s

- 20世纪初的外白渡桥
- Waibaidu Bridge in the 1900s

三

苏州河 Suzhou River

- 外白渡桥边的平静和繁忙
- The quietness and business by the side of Waibaidu Bridge

1907年外白渡桥改为钢桁架桥，这是中国第一座钢结构桥梁，成为上海的符号，被人们称为“外婆桥”

Waibaidu Bridge, reconstructed into a steel truss bridge in 1907, was the first steel structure bridge in China, called "Wai Po Qiao" becoming the symbol of Shanghai

1908 年外白渡桥通行有轨电车

Streetcar passed across Waibaidu Bridge in 1908

三

苏州河 Suzhou River

20世纪20年代的外白渡桥

Waibaidu Bridge in the 1920s

20世纪20年代的外白渡桥

Waibaidu Bridge in the 1920s

20 世纪 30 年代的外白渡桥

Waibaidu Bridge in the 1930s

20 世纪 30 年代的外白渡桥

Waibaidu Bridge in the 1930s

三

苏州河 Suzhou River

● 20 世纪 90 年代的外白渡桥

● Waibaidu Bridge in the 1990s

俯视外白渡桥

Overlooking the Waibaidu Bridge

外白渡桥夜景

Waibaidu Bridge at night

三 苏州河 Suzhou River

从苏州河看外滩源

Seeing Headstream of the Bund from Suzhou River

从苏州河看外滩源

Seeing Headstream of the Bund from Suzhou River

● 外白渡桥南堍，建于1872年的英国领事馆

● The British Consulate built in 1872 was located on the south side of Waibaidu Bridge

● 20世纪50年代英国领事馆旧址

● The old site of British Consulate in the 1950s

三

苏州河 Suzhou River

大清朱家角邮局

20 世纪初外白渡桥北堍

The north side of Waibaidu Bridge in the 1900s

1907 年礼查饭店重建新楼

A new building of Richard Hotel was erected in 1907

● 1916 年建成的俄罗斯领事馆

● Russian Consulate built in 1916

● 1934 年建成的百老汇大厦，1951 年改称上海大厦

● Broadway Mansion built in 1934 was renamed Shanghai Mansion in 1951

三

苏州河 Suzhou River

20 世纪 80 年代苏州河远景

A distant view of Suzhou River in 1980s

1991 年建成的吴淞路闸桥

Wusong Road Gate Bridge built in 1991

● 相隔百年的划船赛

● Two boat races at intervals of a hundred year

三

苏州河 Suzhou River

20世纪初苏州河繁忙的水运商号

The busy waterway transportations along Suzhou River in the 1900s

20世纪初苏州河繁忙的水运商号

The busy waterway transportations along Suzhou River in the 1900s

● 沿岸密集的仓库堆栈和各类工厂，形成了苏州河的工业带

● Warehouses and all kinds of factories packed on the coasts formed the industrial strip of Suzhou River

三 苏州河 Suzhou River

● 北苏州河路旧景

● The old scene on North Suzhou River Road

● 北苏州河路旧景

● The old scene on North Suzhou River Road

南苏州河路旧景

The old scene on South Suzhou River Road

南苏州河路旧景

The old scene on South Suzhou River Road

三 苏州河 Suzhou River

● 苏州河上停泊的船只

● Boats berthed on Suzhou River

● 1905年建于苏州河南岸的划船总会

● Shanghai Rowing Club built on the south bank of Suzhou River in 1905

3 苏州河 Suzhou River

苏州河上的渡船

Ferryboats on Suzhou River

苏州河上停泊的船只

Boats berthed on Suzhou River

三

苏州河

Suzhou River

● 建于1885年的基督教新天安堂

● Christian Union Church built in 1885

● 苏州河边的新天安堂远眺

● A distant view of Christian Union Church on Suzhou River

3 苏州河 Suzhou River

● 兰心大戏院为上海第一座西式剧场，此为1874年重建的砖木结构剧场。位于今圆明园路

● Lyceum Theatre was the first western style theatre in Shanghai and this was the half-timbered theatre rebuilt in 1874 on today's Yuanmingyuan Road.

● 1928年建于虎丘路的光陆大戏院

● Guanglu Theatre built on Huqiu Road in 1928

三 苏州河 Suzhou River

- 建于1876年的二摆渡桥，现为乍浦路桥
- No.2 Baidu Bridge built in 1876 is today's Zhapu Road Bridge

- 1927年二摆渡桥改建成水泥桥
- No.2 Baidu Bridge was reconstructed into a concrete bridge in 1927

● 1890年在里摆渡桥（现四川路桥）南堍东侧建华人公园，供中国人免费游览。

● Chinese Park built in the east of the south side of the Inner Baidu Bridge in 1890 was a free touring place for Chinese.

● 华人公园旧景

● The old scene of Chinese Park

三

苏州河 Suzhou River

- 创建于1864年的公济医院，1877年迁至苏州河北岸
- General Hospital built in 1864 was moved to the north bank of Suzhou River in 1877

- 苏州河北岸公济医院远眺
- A distant view of General Hospital on the north bank of Suzhou River

- 1945 年公济医院改作公立医院
- General Hospital was changed into a public hospital in 1945

- 1953 年公济医院改名为上海市第一人民医院
- General Hospital was renamed as Shanghai First People's Hospital in 1953

三

苏州河 Suzhou River

1875 年建成的里摆渡桥，现为四川路桥

The Inner Baidu Bridge built in 1875 is today's Sichuan Road Bridge

1922 年四川路桥改建成水泥桥

The Sichuan Road Bridge was reconstructed into a concrete bridge in 1922

- 20 世纪 30 年代的四川路桥
- Sichuan Road Bridge in the 1930s

- 20 世纪 50 年代的四川路桥
- Sichuan Road Bridge in the 1930s

三 苏州河 Suzhou River

● 建于 1881 年的江西路桥，也称自来水桥

● Jiangxi Road Bridge built in 1881, also called Tap Water Bridge

年水厂正式供水，水塔建在桥南英租界

W plant began to supply water in 1883 and the water tower was b in the British Concession at the south side of the bridge

三

苏州河 Suzhou River

Shanghai – Soochow Creek.　Burr Photo Co., Shanghai.

● 建于1875年的三摆渡桥，桥北有天后宫庙和吴淞铁路车站，故习称天后宫桥或铁马路桥。1925年改建成水泥桥，现为河南路桥

● The No.3 Baidu Bridge built in 1875 whose north side was Tianhougong Temple and Wusong Railway station was commonly known as Tianhougong Bridge or Iron Road Bridge. It was reconstructed into a concrete bridge in 1925 which is today's Henan Road Bridge

67　Shanse Road in Shanghai.

● 山西路桥，也称盆汤弄桥，建于1885年，1956年拆除

● Shanxi Road Bridge, also called Pengtanglong Bridge, was built in 1885 and removed in 1956

建于 1864 年的老闸吊桥

The Old Sluice Bridge built in 1864

1885 年老闸吊桥改建为福建路木桥，桥左侧的三层楼建筑为安记洋行堆栈

The Old Sluice Bridge was rebuilt into Fujian Road Wood Bridge in 1885. The three-storey building at the left side was the freight house of An Ji foreign firm

三

苏州河 Suzhou River

建于1879年的木桥俗称垃圾桥，1908年重建为钢桁架桥，1942年改称浙江路桥

The wooden bridge built in 1879 was commonly called Lese Bridge. It was rebuilt into a steel truss bridge in 1908 and was renamed Zhejiang Road Bridge in 1942

浙江路桥

Zhejiang Road Bridge

北泥城木桥建于1853年，1899年重建后称西藏路桥，桥南为1864年建成的上海第一个煤气厂

North Nicheng Bridge built in 1853 was rebuilt and renamedas Xizang Road Bridge in 1899 whose south side was the first gasworks in Shanghai built in 1864

桥北有建于1932年的四行仓库，1937年在此留下"八百壮士"的英勇战迹

The north side of the bridge was Sihang Warehouse built in 1932. "The Eight Hundred Heroes" fought bravely here in 1937

三

苏州河 Suzhou River

● 苏州河上的拱桥

● The arch bridge on Suzhou River

● 苏州河上的拱桥

● The arch bridge on Suzhou River

● 1931 年建成的宝成桥，习称谈家渡桥

● Baocheng Bridge built in 1931 is commonly known as Tanjiadu Bridge

● 建于 1995 年的南北高架道路桥

● South–North Road Flyover built in 1995

三
苏州河 Suzhou River

建于清末的极司非而公园

Jessfield Park built in the late Qing Dynasty

极司非而公园又称梵王渡公园

Jessfield Park was also called Fanwangdu Park

● 1914 年改名兆丰公园

● It was renamed as Zhaofeng Park in 1914

● 1942 年改名中山公园

● It was renamed as Zhongshan Park in 1942

三
苏州河
Suzhou River

20世纪40年代的中山公园

Zhongshan Park in the 1940s

20世纪70年代的中山公园

Zhongshan Park in the 1970s

21 世纪初的中山公园一角

A corner of Zhongshan Park in the 2000s

1922 年建成的上海造币厂，位于今江宁路桥北堍

Shanghai Mint built in 1922 was located on today's north side of Jiangning Road Bridge

三

苏州河 Suzhou River

● 1879年圣约翰学院创建于苏州河畔，现为华东政法学院

● Saint John's College built on the bank of Suzhou River in 1879 is today's East China University of Politics and Law

● 校园内的建筑

● The building in the campus

● 建于1898年的校长办公楼，曾为上海社会科学院办公楼

● The president's building built in 1898 was once the office building of Shanghai Academy of Social Sciences

21世纪初的华东政法学院校园

The campus of East China University of Politics and Law in the 2000s

21世纪初的华东政法学院校园

The campus of East China University of Politics and Law in the 2000s

● 创建于1924年的大夏大学，现为华东师范大学

● Daxia University established in 1924 is today's East China Normal University

● 校园内的丽娃河与苏州河碧水相连

● The Liwa River in the campus links with Suzhou River

三

苏州河 Suzhou River

● 20世纪40年代的苏州河

● Suzhou River in the 1940s

● 20世纪50年代的苏州河

● Suzhou River in the 1950s

20世纪60年代的苏州河

Suzhou River in the 1960s

20世纪70年代的苏州河

Suzhou River in the 1970s

三

苏州河 Suzhou River

20世纪80年代的苏州河

Suzhou River in the 1980s

20世纪90年代的苏州河

Suzhou River in the 1990s

21 世纪初的苏州河

Suzhou River in the 2000s

● 1998年实施苏州河治理工程，黑臭的水浜变成了清澈宜人的河道

● The management project of Suzhou River was implemented in 1998. Black and smelly water became the clean river way

三

苏州河 Suzhou River

大清朱家角邮局

● 清澈的苏州河

● The clean Suzhou River

苏州河的春天

Suzhou River in springtime

苏州河的春天

Suzhou River in springtime

三

苏州河 Suzhou River

● 苏州河两岸新貌

● The new look of the two sides of Suzhou River

四

外　　滩

The Bund

外滩是外黄浦滩的简称。广义的外滩，不仅指过去英租界的临江段，还包括法租界、美租界的现称为南、北外滩的范围。19世纪初期，这里是一片芦苇丛生的浅滩，只有一条船夫拉纤的小路。1845年这块区域被划定为第一块英租界。1849年英国领事馆从县城迁至黄浦江与苏州河交界的李家场，此处成为外滩的发源地。一百多年过去了，外滩由早期的码头堆栈发展到拥有风格迥异的“万国建筑”而展示了其特有的城市风貌。外滩已成为上海的标志。

The Bund is a short name for the bund of Huangpu River. Generally speaking, the Bund not only includes the area near the river which belonged to the former British Concession but also the current South Bund and the North Bund which belonged to the French Concession. In the early 19th century, it was a shoal with reeds where there was only one small road for the boatmen to track the boats. In 1845, this area was designated as the first land of the British Concession. In 1849, the British Consulate moved from the county to Lijiachang, the border of Huangpu River and Suzhou River, which became the cradleland of the Bund. During more than one hundred years, from the early wharves to today's mingled international architectures, the Bund showed the special flavor of the city and it has become the symbol of Shanghai.

四 外滩 The Bund

● 19 世纪末的外滩

● The Bund in the late 19th century

● 19 世纪末的外滩

● The Bund in the late 19th century

● 外滩月弯形的江面是泊船的天然良港

● The meniscus shaped surface of the Bund was a natural harbor for mooring

● 1853 年外滩已有十余座驳船码头

● There were more than 10 barge berths on the Bund in 1853

四 外滩 The Bund

1872 年重建的英国领事馆，是外滩源保存最早的外国建筑

British Consulate General reconstructed in 1872 was the earliest preserved foreign building in Headstream of the Bund

英国领事馆

British Consulate General

20世纪初的外滩源

Headstream of the Bund in the 1900s

20世纪90年代的外滩源

Headstream of the Bund in the 1990s

四 外滩 The Bund

- 随潮水带来的泥沙在这里淤积
- Mud and sand which were brought by tidewater deposit here

- 外滩花园的地基就是由泥沙淤积而形成的
- The foundation of the Bund Garden was formed by the sediment of mud and sand

● 黄浦江与苏州河的交汇处

● The intersection of Huangpu River and Suzhou River

● 黄浦江与苏州河的交汇处

● The intersection of Huangpu River and Suzhou River

● 外滩花园1868年建成，也称公家花园，是中国第一座公共园林

● The Bund Garden built in 1868, also called Public Garden, was the first public park in China

● 1905年公家花园大门改建，由西北方向迁至今朝南位置

● The gate of the Public Garden was reconstructed in 1905 and changed its direction from the northwest to today's south direction

● 公家花园音乐亭雪景

● Snowscape of the Music Pavilion in the Public Garden

● 在音乐亭举办音乐会

● A concert was held in the Music Pavilion

四 外滩 The Bund

公家花园旧景

The old scene of the Public Garden

公家花园1886年以前只对与中国签约国的侨民开放，不允许中国人入内

Before 1886, the Public Garden was only open to the nationals of China's signatory countries and the Chinese were not allowed to enter

公家花园旧景

The old scene of the Public Garden

公家花园旧景

The old scene of the Public Garden

四 外滩 The Bund

1928年公家花园对中国人开放

The Public Garden was open to the Chinese People in 1928

20世纪30年代的公家花园

The Public Garden in the 1930s

- 1949 年公家花园改名为黄浦公园
- The Public Garden was renamed as Huangpu Park in 1949

- 20 世纪 50 年代的黄浦公园
- Huangpu Park in the 1950s

四

外滩 The Bund

20 世纪 70 年代的黄浦公园

Huangpu Park in the 1970s

20 世纪 90 年代的黄浦公园，1994 年上海人民英雄纪念塔建成

Huangpu Park in the 1990s. Shanghai People's Hero Memorial Column was built in 1994

● 1864年建于公家花园北门的“常胜军”纪念碑（李鸿章为纪念围剿太平军的洋枪队所建），1942年被拆除

● The monument to memorize the Ever Victorious Army built near the north gate of the Public Garden in 1864 was removed in 1942. (Li Hongzhang built it in commemoration of members of the army which encircled and suppressed the Taiping army)

● 1880年英国在北门外建的马嘉理纪念碑（马嘉理是被中国人击毙的英国领事馆翻译），1942年被拆除

● Margary Monument built by Britain outside the north gate in 1880 was removed in 1942. (Margary was a translator in the British Consulate General who was shot dead by Chinese)

● 外白渡桥与公家花园相邻，故也称花园桥、公园桥

● Waibaidu Bridge was adjacent to Public Garden, so it was called Garden Bridge or Park Bridge

● 20世纪初的外白渡桥南堍

● The southern side of Waibaidu Bridge in the 1900s

20世纪10年代的外白渡桥南堍

The southern side of Waibaidu Bridge in the 1910s

20世纪30年代的外白渡桥南堍

The southern side of Waibaidu Bridge in the 1930s

四 外滩 The Bund

● 19世纪末外滩的两个建筑

● The two buildings on the Bund in the late 19th century

● 建于1856年的外洋泾桥

● Waiyangjing Bridge built in 1856

1898 年建于外滩的伊尔底斯纪念碑（德国为纪念其海军伊尔底斯号炮舰在中国黄海沉没全体船员遇难而建），1929 年迁移，1959 年拆除

Iltis Monument built on the Bund in 1898 was moved in 1929 and removed in 1959. (Germany built it in commemoration of the wreck of its naval gunboat named Iltis which sank in Huanghai, China)

伊尔底斯纪念碑

Iltis monument

四

外滩 The Bund

20世纪初的外滩堤岸

The bank of the Bund in the 1900s

20世纪初的外滩堤岸

The bank of the Bund in the 1900s

外滩沿江旧景

The old riverine scene of the Bund

外滩沿江旧景

The old riverine scene of the Bund

四 外滩 The Bund

20世纪初的外滩景观

Landscape of the Bund in the 1900s

20世纪初的外滩景观

Landscape of the Bund in the 1900s

1908 年的外滩雪景

The snowscape on the Bund in 1908

外滩雪景

The snowscape on the Bund

四 外滩 The Bund

1896 年在外滩开业的华俄道胜银行，是中国第一家中外合资银行

Russo–Chinese Bank opened on the Bund in 1896 was the first joint Chinese–foreign bank in China

外滩早期的洋行多为二、三层建筑

Most of the buildings of the early foreign firms on the Bund own two or three storeys

早期的外滩道路

The early road of the Bund

早期的外滩道路

The early road of the Bund

四

外滩

The Bund

● 外滩的草坪

● The lawn of the Bund

● 外滩的草坪

● The lawn of the Bund

- 行驶在外滩的各种人力车
- The rickshaws running on the Bund

- 行驶在外滩的各种车辆
- All kinds of vehicles running on the Bund

四 外滩 The Bund

大清朱家角郵局

● 外滩成为人们游览的场所

● The Bund became a place for sightseeing

在外滩往来的各国行人

Pedestrians from various countries walking on the Bund

四

外滩 The Bund

1899年的外滩（现北京东路口）

The Bund in 1899 at the crossing of East Beijing Road

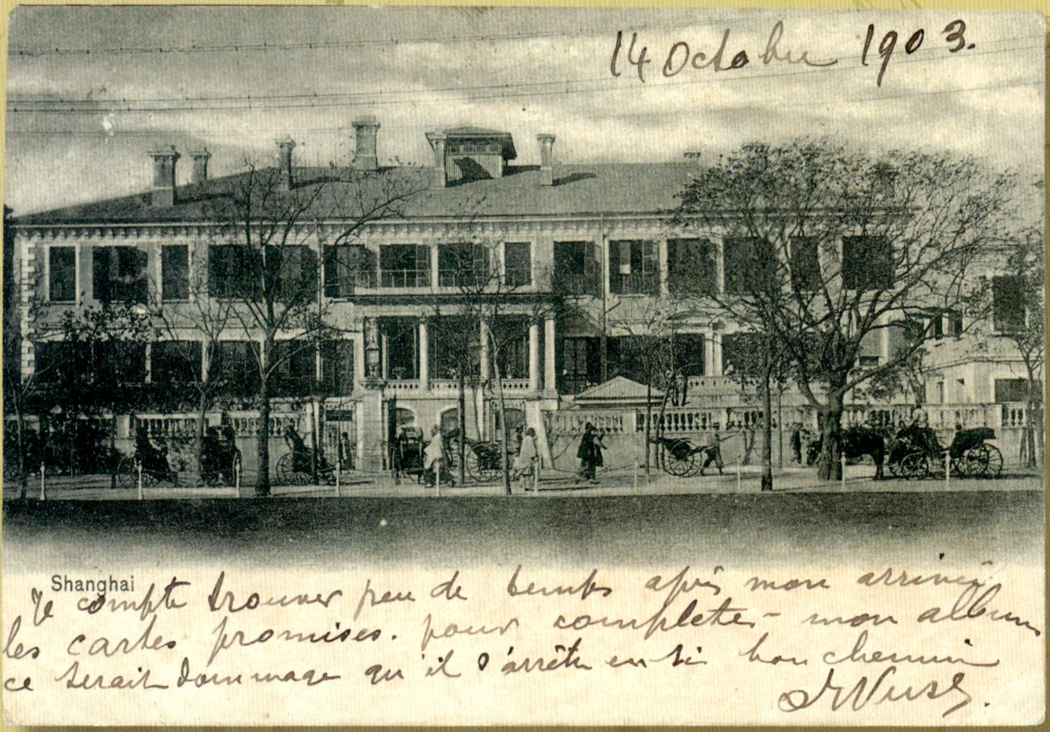

建于1843年的怡和洋行

Jardine Matheson built in 1843

1922年怡和洋行重建新楼

The new building of Jardine Matheson was reconstructed in 1922

1983年加层改建后的外贸大楼

Foreign Trade Building was reconstructed by adding floors in 1983

● 建于1893年的日本横滨正金银行

● Yokohama Special Bank of Japan built in 1893

● 建于1907年的德国总会，"一战"后被中国接收改为中国银行

● German Club established in 1907 was taken over by China as Bank of China after WWI

● 1928年中国银行左侧建成华懋饭店，又称沙逊大厦

● Cathay Hotel, also called Sassoon House, was built in 1928 on the left side of Bank of China

● 1937 年重建的中国银行大厦

● The building of Bank of China was reconstructed in 1937

四

外滩 The Bund

● 1902年外滩（现南京东路口），左侧为中央饭店，1903年改为汇中饭店

● The Bund at the crossing of Nanjing Road in 1902. The left side was the Central Hotel which was renamed Palace Hotel in 1903

● 建于1894年的英国驻华公使巴夏礼塑像

● Statue of Sir Harry Smith Parkes, Britannic Majesty's Ambassador to the People's Republic of China was built in 1894

● 1908年汇中饭店重建，成为中国第一栋使用电梯的建筑。1909年在此举行世界第一次万国禁烟会。1911年12月25日，孙中山曾在此作总统就职前演讲

● The Palace Hotel was reconstructed in 1908 becoming the first building with elevator in China. The world's first International Anti-Opium Commission was held here in 1909. On December 25th, 1911, Sun Yat-sen made a speech here before he took office

● 1956年沙逊大厦改称和平饭店，1965年汇中饭店并入和平饭店。陈毅市长塑像建于1993年

● Sassoon House was renamed Peace Hotel in 1956 and in 1965 Huizhong Hotel merged into it. The statue of the former mayor Chen Yi was built in 1993

四 外滩 The Bund

中间建筑为早期的麦加利银行和字林洋行。字林洋行于1864年创办字林西报

The building in the middle was the early Chartered Bank of India, Australia and China and North-China Herald Office. North China Daily News was started by North-China Herald Office in 1864

1914年建于外滩的赫德塑像，英国人赫德创立了中国邮政，执掌海关大权48年

Monument of Hart was built on the Bund in 1914. Hart, a British, founded China Post and owned the power to run the Customs for 48 years

● 1923 年重建的字林西报大楼为当时外滩最高的建筑

● North China Daily News Building, the highest building on the Bund that time was rebuilt in 1923

● 20 世纪 20 年代重建的麦加利银行和台湾银行

● Chartered Bank of India, Australia and China and Taiwan Bank rebuilt in the 1920s

1910 年重建的华俄道胜银行

Shanghai-Russo Chinese Bank was reconstructed in 1910

1994 年在此建立中国外汇交易中心

China Foreign Exchange Center was established here in 1994

● 建于1890年的德华银行，"一战"后被中国接收改为交通银行

● Deutsche—Asiatische Bank built in 1890 was taken over by China as Bank of Communications after WWI

● 1940年交通银行重建新楼，现为上海市总工会

● The new building of Bank of Communications was reconstructed in 1940 which is the current Shanghai Municipal Federation of the Unions

● 位于老城厢东北黄浦江边的江海大关

● Chinese Customs was located on the northeast side of the Old Town and the side of Huangpu River

● 1857 年在外滩建中国传统式新关，称江海北关

● The Chinese traditional customs called North Customs was built on the Bund in 1857

● 1893 年重建西洋式有钟楼的江海北关

● The western style North Customs with a bell tower was rebuilt in 1893

● 1927 年再次重建现代风格的海关大楼

● The Customs House with modern style was rebuilt once more in 1927

四
外滩 The Bund

1874年建于外滩的汇丰银行

HSBC built on the Bund in 1874

外滩的汇丰银行

HSBC on the Bund

● 1923 年重建的汇丰大楼，是上海第一座使用空调的建筑

● HSBC Building reconstructed in 1923 was the first building using air conditioner in Shanghai

● 1955 年至 1995 年，汇丰大楼为上海市人民政府机关大楼，现为浦东发展银行

● HSBC Building was the office building of Shanghai Municipal People's Government from 1955 to 1995. It is today's Pudong Development Bank

四 外滩 The Bund 大清朱家角邮局

● 左起第一、第二座建筑分别为大北电报公司、轮船招商局大楼。成立于1872年的轮船招商局是中国最早的航运企业，中国的第一部公用电话和最早的电话交换机曾在大北电报公司使用

● The first and second buildings are the buildings of China Merchants Steamship Navigation Company and Great Northern Telegraph. China Merchants Steamship Navigation Company started in 1872 was the earliest shipping enterprise in China. The first public phone and the earliest telephone switchboard in China were used in the Great Northern Telegraph Company

● 大北电报公司大楼现为盘古银行

● The building of Great Northern Telegraph is Bangkok Bank

● 右起第一座建筑为1897年成立的中国通商银行，是近代中国自办的第一家银行

● The first building from the right side is the Commercial Bank of China established in 1897 which was the first self-owned bank in China in modern times

● 保持原貌的日清轮船公司和有利银行大楼

● Nissin shipping company and You Li building maintain the original appearance

四 外滩 The Bund

SHANGHAI CLUB.

THE BUND AND SHANGHAI CLUB

● 建于1864年的英国总会是上海的第一家外侨俱乐部

● Britain Club established in 1864 is the first alien club in Shanghai

● 1909年重建的总会大楼，为上海第一座钢筋水泥建筑

● The building was reconstructed in 1909 which was the first armored concrete building in Shanghai

大清朱家角郵局

● 总会俱乐部前停泊的船只

● Ships berthed in front of the club

● 清末总会俱乐部大楼外景

● The outdoor scene of the building of the club in the late Qing Dynasty

民国时期总会俱乐部大楼外景

The outdoor scene of the building of the club in the Republic Period

民国时期总会俱乐部大楼外景

The outdoor scene of the building of the club in the Republic Period

1956 年改建为国际海员俱乐部

It was reconstructed and became the International Seamen's Club in 1956

1971 年更名为东风饭店

The name was changed to East Wind Hotel in 1971

四

外滩 The Bund

建于1916年的亚细亚火油公司大楼

The building of Asiatic Petroleum Company was built in 1916

1884年外滩兴建信号台，为进港船只提供气象信息

The signal station was built on the Bund in 1884 to provide meteorological information for ships that entered the harbor

● 早期的木杆信号台建于外滩洋泾浜右侧

● The early signal beacon made of wooden pole was built at the right side of Yangjingbang on the Bund

● 洋泾浜为英法租界的界河，1915 年填平筑路，称爱多亚路

● Yangjingbang was the boundary river of the British Concession and French Concession which was filled to pave road and called Avenue Edward in 1915

四

外滩 The Bund

大清朱家角邮局

● 1907年重建水泥结构的信号塔

● The cement structure signal beacon was reconstructed in 1907

20世纪20年代的信号塔

The signal beacon in the 1920s

20世纪20年代的信号塔

The signal beacon in the 1920s

四

外滩 The Bund

大清朱家角郵局

20 世纪 50 年代的信号塔

The signal beacon in the 1950s

1993 年信号塔被整体向东移位 20 米

The whole signal beacon was moved about 20 meters to the east in 1993

● 1924年欧战纪念碑在外滩建成，也称女神纪念碑。1942年该碑被拆除，后建成过江轮渡站

● The Monument of Victory, also called the Statue of Peace, was built on the Bund in 1924. The monument was removed in 1942 and converted to a river steamer station afterwards

20世纪初的法租界外滩

The French Bund in the 1900s

20世纪初的法租界外滩

The French Bund in the 1900s

1854 年法国领事馆迁至外滩

French Consulate moved to the Bund in 1854

建于 1895 年的法国领事馆，1987 年被拆除，1993 年建成光明大厦

French Consulate built in 1895 was removed in 1987 and became the Light Building in 1993

四 外滩 The Bund 大清朱家角邮局

1874 年人工开凿的新开河，1908 年填平

Man-made Xinkaihe built in 1874 was filled in 1908

建于法租界外滩路上的新开河桥

Xinkaihe Bridge built on the Bund in the French Concession

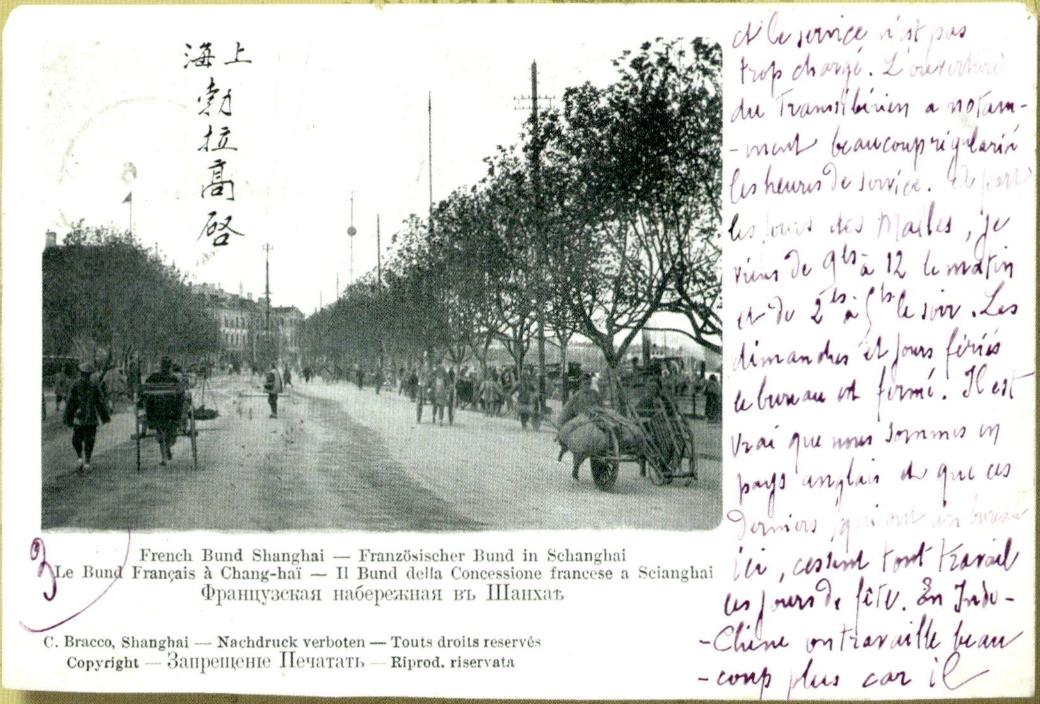

早期的法租界道路

The early road in the French Concession

早期的法租界道路

The early road in the French Concession

● 建于 1866 年的法国火轮码头

● French ship wharf built in 1866

大清朱家角邮局

● 建于 1862 年的金利源码头

● Jinliyuan wharf built in 1862

● 行驶在法租界外滩的电车

● The street car running on the Bund in the French concession

20世纪10年代的南外滩

The South Bund in the 1910s

20世纪10年代的外滩爱多亚路路口

The Bund in the 1910s at the crossing of Edward Avenue

20世纪20年代的南外滩

The South Bund in the 1920s

20世纪20年代的南外滩

The South Bund in the 1920s

四

外滩 The Bund

20世纪30年代的南外滩

The South Bund in the 1930s

20世纪30年代的南外滩

The South Bund in the 1930s

20 世纪 90 年代的外滩延安东路口

The Bund in the 1990s at the crossing of East Yan'an Road

21 世纪初的南外滩夜景

The night scene of the South Bund in the 2000s

● 礼查饭店是外侨在上海创办的第一家西洋饭店，于1860年迁址黄浦路，是上海最早使用电灯、电话的饭店

● Richard Hotel, the first western hotel in Shanghai held by aliens moved to Huangpu Road in 1860 which was the earliest hotel using electric light and the telephone

● 1910年礼查饭店重建。1922年爱因斯坦来上海在此居住，并获知自己提出的“广义相对论”荣获了该年度的诺贝尔物理奖

● Richard Hotel was reconstructed in 1910. Einstein came to Shanghai in 1922 and lived here during which period he leart that his general theory of relativity won the Nobel Physics prize that year

1916 年在礼查饭店前建成俄罗斯领事馆

Consulate General of the Russian Federation was built in front of Richard Hotel in 1916

1959 年礼查饭店改称浦江饭店，1990 年 12 月 19 日上海证券交易所在浦江饭店挂牌成立

Richard Hotel was renamed Pujiang Hotel in 1959. On December 19th, 1990, the Shanghai Securities Exchange was founded in Pujiang Hotel

- 1854 年美国领事馆迁址黄浦路
- American Consulate moved to Huangpu Road in 1854

- 1861 年德国在黄浦路建领事署，1878 年升格为领事馆
- Germany built a Bureau of Consular Affairs on Huangpu Road in 1861 which became a consulate in 1878

● 建于 1884 年的德国领事馆，1982 年被拆除后建海鸥饭店

● The German Consulate built in 1884 was removed in 1982 and the site became Seagull Hotel later

上海外白渡桥

● 1984 年建成的海鸥饭店

● Seagull Hotel built in 1984

四 外滩 The Bund

● 早期的北外滩建筑

● The early buildings on the North Bund

● 早期的北外滩建筑

● The early buildings on the North Bund

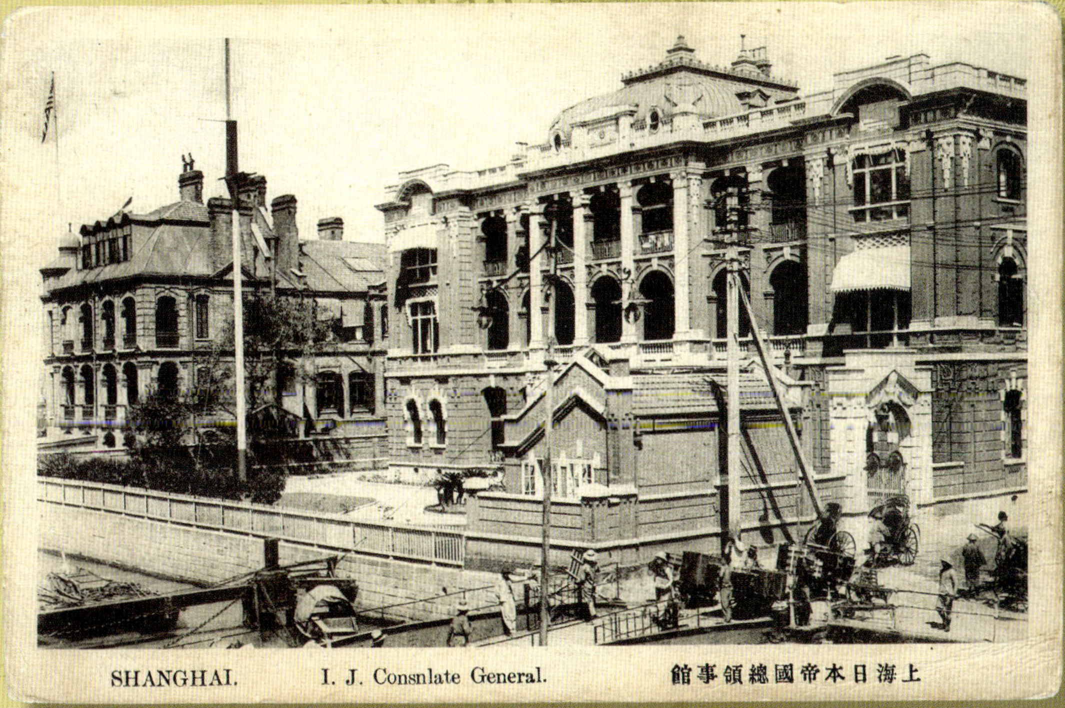

- 建于1870年的日本领事馆
- Japanese Consulate built in 1870

- 1870年兴建的日本邮船会社
- Nippon Yusen Kaisha (NYK) built in 1870

四 外滩 The Bund

邮船码头

Wharf for mooring postboats

虹口港和沿江码头

Hongkou port and the riverine wharf

20 世纪 20 年代的北外滩

The North Bund in the 1920s

20 世纪 20 年代的北外滩

The North Bund in the 1920s

四

外滩 The Bund

● 20 世纪 90 年代的北外滩
● The North Bund in the 1990s

● 20 世纪 90 年代的北外滩
● The North Bund in the 1990s

19 世纪末的外滩

The Bund in the late 19th Century

19 世纪末的外滩

The Bund in the late 19th Century

四

外滩 The Bund

20 世纪初的外滩

The Bund in the 1900s

20 世纪初的外滩

The Bund in the 1900s

● 20 世纪 10 年代的外滩

● The Bund in the 1910s

● 20 世纪 10 年代的外滩

● The Bund in the 1910s

四
外滩
The Bund

20 世纪 20 年代的外滩
The Bund in the 1920s

20 世纪 20 年代的外滩
The Bund in the 1920s

20世纪30年代的外滩

The Bund in the 1930s

20世纪30年代的外滩

The Bund in the 1930s

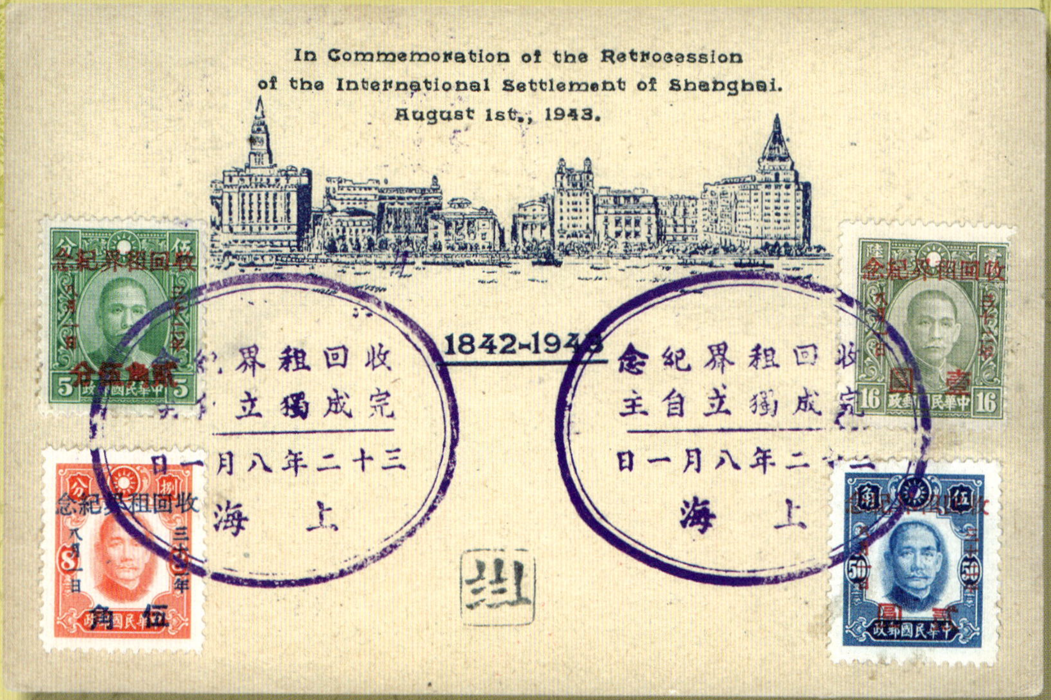

20世纪40年代的外滩

The Bund in the 1940s

20世纪40年代的外滩

The Bund in the 1940s

20世纪50年代的外滩

The Bund in the 1950s

20世纪50年代的外滩

The Bund in the 1950s

20世纪60年代的外滩

The Bund in the 1960s

20世纪60年代的外滩

The Bund in the 1960s

20世纪70年代的外滩

The Bund in the 1970s

20世纪70年代的外滩

The Bund in the 1970s

四 外滩 The Bund

20世纪80年代的外滩

The Bund in the 1980s

20世纪80年代的外滩

The Bund in the 1980s

20世纪90年代前期的外滩

The Bund in the early 1990s

20世纪90年代前期的外滩

The Bund in the early 1990s

20 世纪 90 年代后期的外滩

The Bund in the late 1990s

20 世纪 90 年代后期的外滩

The Bund in the late 1990s

21 世纪初的外滩

The Bund in the 2000s

21 世纪初的外滩

The Bund in the 2000s

四

外滩 The Bund

外滩江堤成为观光平台

The enbarkment of the Bund became a sightseeing platform

1992年和平饭店被国际组织列为世界著名饭店

Peace Hotel was listed as a world famous hotel by the international organization in 1992

外滩远眺

A bistant view of the Bund

延安路高架外滩下匝道，2008 年被拆除

The off-ramp of Yan'an Road Viaduct was removed in 2008

2009年吴淞路闸桥被拆除，形成苏州河滨水绿地

Wusong Road Sluice Bridge was removed in 2009 and the green area of Suzhou Riverside has formed

2010年新建的外滩观景平台

Sight-seeing Platform newly built on the Bund in 2010

2010年外滩建成以气象信号台为中心的延安路广场

Yan'an Road Square built in 2010 with the meteorological signal station at the center

2010年综合改造工程完成后的外滩新貌

New face of the Bund after the completion of the comprehensive renovation project in 2010

21 世纪初的外滩夜色

The night scene of the Bund in the 2000s

21 世纪初的外滩夜色

The night scene of the Bund in the 2000s

五

南　京　路

Nanjing Road

南京路是1845年英租界建立后筑成的第一条马路，现包括南京东路和南京西路，东起外滩，西至延安西路，全长5.5公里。南京路伴随着跑马场的三次变迁而延伸，是一条遛马走出来的路。早在19世纪末，南京路已成为上海的商业中心，有许多的第一从这里开始，由此改变着人们的观念和习惯。世界多样性的交流，使南京路始终走在时世的前沿，充满了活力和光彩。南京路被誉为中华商业第一街，并以繁华著称于世。

Nanjing Road is the first road paved after the establishment of the British Concession in 1845. Now it covers East Nanjing Road and West Nanjing Road starting from the Bund in the east and ending at West Yan'An Road with a length of five and a half kilometers. Extending with the changes of the horse race ring for three times, it is a road formed by walking horses. Since the late 19th century, Nanjing Road had already become the commercial center of Shanghai. There were many firsts which changed people's notion and habit. The multifarious intercommunion in the world has placed Nanjing Road in the forefront of the times with vitality and radiance. Nanjing Road is praised as the first commercial street in China and is world-famous for its prosperity.

五

南京路 Nanjing Road

1917年上海英租界分图

The detail drawing of the British Concession in Shanghai in 1917

这条马路曾称派克弄、花园路

This road was once called Park Lane and Garden Road

5

南京路 Nanjing Road

● 又称英大马路，1865 年更名为南京路

● It was also referred as the British Main Road and renamed Nanjing Road in 1856

● 南京路旧景

● The old scene of Nanjing Road

五 南京路 Nangjing Road

1850年在路左侧河南路五圣庙建第一跑马场，也称抛球场

The first forse race ring was built on the left side of the road—Wushengmiao on He'nan Road in 1850

1854年在路右侧湖北路、北海路一带建第二跑马场

The second forse race ring was built on the right side of the road—Hubei Road and Beihai Road area

1865 年南京路始装煤气灯，此处为广西路口

The gas lamp was first equipped on Nanjing Road in 1865 and this is the crossing of Guangxi Road

1882 年南京路更换电灯

The electric light replaced gas light on Nanjing Road in 1882

五

南京路 Nangjing Road

19世纪末南京路街景

Streetscape of Nanjing Road in the late 19th century

19世纪末南京路街景

Streetscape of Nanjing Road in the late 19th century

20 世纪初的南京路仍是一条泥土街道

Nanjing Road was still a street full of clay in the 1900s

1901 年清醇亲王载沣乘轿经过南京路

The 2nd Prince Chun of Qing Dynasty Zaifeng passed Nanjing Road sitting in a sedan chair in 1901

五 南京路 Nanjing Road

● 南京路上的马车与人力车

● Carriages and rickshaws on Nanjing Road

● 1908 年南京路上行驶有轨电车

● The streetcars ran on Nanjing Road in 1908

5 南京路 Nanjing Road

- 20世纪初南京路上的酱园与药铺
- The condiment shop and herbal medicine shop on Nanjing Road in the 1900s

五 南京路 Nanjing Road

1870年邵万生南货店迁至南京路

Shaowansheng Store of Southern Specialties moved to Nanjing Road in 1870

南京路上的药铺

Pharmacies on Nanjing Road

● 南京路上的全安茶楼

● The Quan An Tea House on Nanjing Road

● 南京路上的易安茶楼

● Yi An Tea House on Nanjing Road

五

南京路 Nanjing Road

南京路上的茶楼和店铺

Teahouses and Shops on Nanjing Road

1914年拆除易安等茶楼兴建先施公司，现为时装公司和东亚饭店

The Teahouses like Yi An were removed in 1914 and the Sincere Company Limited was established which is today's Fashion Company and East Asia Hotel

太阳啤酒与王宝和酒店

Sun beer and Wang Baohe Restaurant

南京路旧景

The old scene of Nanjing Road

五

南京路 Nanjing Road

● 庆和银楼与费文元银楼

● Qinghe Jewelry shop and Fei Wenyuan Jewelry shop

● 建于1896年的工部局市政厅，1911年南北议和在此举行。1929年被拆除，以后建成新雅粤菜馆

● Municipal Committee Hall established in 1896 was removed in 1929 where the Peace Negotiation between North and South was held in 1911 and it was rebuilt as Xinya Cantonese Restaurant later

● 工部局市政厅

● Municipal Committee Hall

五

南京路 Nanging Road

大清朱家角郵局

邮电局

Post and Telecommunications Office

文明书局

Civilization Press

● 1930 年老凤祥银楼迁至南京路

● Laofengxiang jewelry store moved to Nanjing Road in 1930

● 老凤祥银楼与交通银行

● Laofengxiang jewelry store and Bank of Communications

五

南京路 Nanjing Road

大清朱家角邮局

外滩南京路口

The Bund at the east crossing of Nanjing Road

外滩南京路口

The Bund at the east crossing of Nanjing Road

● 20 世纪 30 年代南京路口

● The east crossing of Nanjing Road in the 1930s

● 20 世纪 30 年代南京路口

● The east crossing of Nanjing Road in the 1930s

五

南京路 Nanjing Road

南京路东段街景

The street scene of the east part of Nanjing Road

大清朱家角郵局

南京路东段街景

The street scene of the east part of Nanjing Road

● 南京路东段为早期的商业中心，惠罗、福利、汇司、泰兴被称为“前四大公司”

● The eastern section of Nanjing Road was the early business center. Whiteaway, Laidlaw & Co. Ltd., Hall, Haltz & Co. Ltd., Weeks & Co. Ltd. and Lane, Crawford & Co. Ltd. were called the former four companies

● 惠罗公司和福利公司

● Whiteaway, Laidlaw & Co. Ltd. and Hall, Haltz & Co. Ltd.

20世纪初的南京路浙江路口

The crossing of Nanjing Road and Zhejiang Road in the 1900s

南京路浙江路口宝成裕记银楼

Baocheng Yu Ji Jewelry shop on the intersection of Nanjing Road and Zhejiang Road

20 世纪 20 年代的南京路

Nanjing Road in the 1920s

20 世纪 20 年代的南京路

Nanjing Road in the 1920s

五

南京路 Nangjing Road

永安公司于1918年建成开业

Wing On Company was built and opened in 1918

1987年改称华联商厦，2005年恢复原名

It was renamed as Shanghai Hualian Co Ltd in 1987 and resumed the former name in 2005

● 新新公司1926年建成，现为第一食品公司。大新公司1936年建成，现为第一百货商店

● Sun Sun Company was established in 1926 which is today's Shanghai First Food Store. Da Sun Co. Ltd. was established in 1936 which is today's First Department Store

● 先施、永安、新新、大新四大公司成为南京路的标志

● The Sincere & Co. Ltd., the Wing On Co. Ltd., the Sun Sun Co. Ltd. and the Da Sun Co. Ltd. were the symbols of Nanjing Road

五

南京路 Nanjing Road

● 20世纪30年代的南京路

● Nanjing Road in the 1930s

● 20世纪30年代的南京路

● Nanjing Road in the 1930s

1937 年 8 月南京路遭日军轰炸

Nanjing Road was bombed by Japanese army in August, 1937

日军轰炸南京路

Nanjing Road was bombed by Japanese army

五

南京路 Nanjing Road

大清朱家角郵局

20世纪40年代的南京路

Nanjing Road in the 1940s

20世纪40年代的南京路

Nanjing Road in the 1940s

● 20世纪30、40年代南京路夜景

● The night scene of Nanjing Road in the 1930s and 1940s

五

南京路 Nanjing Road

图中间为中泥城桥。1914年泥城浜被填平，建成西藏路。陈长福号址现为中百一店

In the middle of the picture is the Middle Nicheng Bridge. The river was filled and paved the road called Xizang Road in 1914. Cheng Changfu Store is now the Shanghai No.1 Department Store

清末南京路劳合路，今为六合路

Lloyd Road and Nanjing Road in the late Qing Dynasty (today's Liuhe Road)

20世纪初南京路西藏路口

The crossing of Nanjing Road and Xizang Road in the 1900s

1910年开设荣昌祥西服号，孙中山在该店定制了第一套“中山装”

Rongchangxiang western-style clothes store was opened in 1910 and Mr. Sun Yat-Sen ordered the first Chinese tunic suit there

五

南京路 Nanjing Road

大清朱家角邮局

前左侧建筑为1915年建成的新世界游乐场，解放后改为黄浦区少年宫和上海精品商厦，已拆除

The front left building was the New World pleasure ground built in 1915 which was changed to the children's hall in Huangpu district and Shanghai Superfine Commercial Building after liberation. And now they have been removed

1918年扩建北部新世界游乐场

The northern New World pleasure ground was extended in 1918

● 荣昌祥店址

● The site of Rongchangxiang western-style clothes store

● 1936 年在荣昌祥店址建成大新公司大楼

● In 1936, the site of Rongchangxiang western-style clothes store was rebuilt as the building of Da Sun Co. Ltd

五

南京路 Nanjing Road

大清朱家角郵局

20世纪30年代的南京路西藏路口

The crossing of Nanjing Road and Xizang Road in the 1930s

20世纪30年代的南京路西藏路口

The crossing of Nanjing Road and Xizang Road in the 1930s

大新公司大楼

The building of Da Sun Co. Ltd

1953年上海市第一百货商店迁至大新公司大楼

The First Department Store of Shanghai was moved to the building of Da Sun Co. Ltd. in 1953

20 世纪 60 年代南京路西藏路口

The crossing of Nanjing Road and Xizang Road in the 1960s

20 世纪 80 年代南京路西藏路口

Nanjing Road in the 1980s at the crossing of Xizang Road

1985年南京路西藏路口建成的人行天桥，现已拆除

The pedestrian bridge built in 1985 at the crossing of Nanjing Road and Xiang Road. Now it has been removed

1995 年建成的新世界城

New World City built in 1995

五

南京路 Nangjing Road

清末时期的南京路

Nanjing Road in the late Qing Dynasty

1911 年辛亥革命上海光复时的南京路

Nanjing Road during the recovery period in the Revolution of 1911

● 民国时期的南京路

● Nanjing Road during the period of Republic of China

● 新中国新世纪的南京路

● Nanjing Road in the new century of New China

五 南京路 Nanjing Road

● 20世纪50年代的南京路，电车轨道于1963年被拆除

● Nanjing Road in the 1950s, The tramways were demolished in 1963

● 1956年和1969年永安公司两次更名为第十百货商店

● Yong An Company changed its name to the tenth Department Store twice in 1956 and 1969

20世纪80年代的南京路

Nanjing Road in the 1980s

五 南京路 Nanjing Road

● 20 世纪 90 年代的南京路

● Nanjing Road in the 1990s

5 南京路 Nanjing Road

1999年建成的南京路步行街

Pedestrian Street of Nanjing Road was built in 1999

五 南京路 Nanjing Road

21 世纪初的南京路

Nanjing Road in the 2000s

21 世纪初的南京路

Nanjing Road in the 2000s

21 世纪初的南京路夜景

The night scene of Nanjing Road in the 2000s

21 世纪初的南京路夜景

The night scene of Nanjing Road in the 2000s

五

南京路 Nanjing Road

● 1861年在西藏路西侧建第三跑马场，也称跑马厅

● The third horse race ring was built on the west side of Xizang Road in 1861, also called Race Course

大清朱家角邮局

● 跑马场静安寺路一侧

● Race Course on the side of Jing' an Temple Road

● 1862 年建成跑马总会大楼

● The building of Shanghai Race Club was built in 1862

● 跑马总会大楼

● The building of Shanghai Race Club

Grand Stand, Race Course, Shanghai

- 跑马场也成为训练、集会等活动场所
- The Race Course is also a place for the activities of training and meeting

"Light Horse", Shanghai.

● 板球俱乐部远景

● A distant view of the cricket club

● 建于跑马场的板球俱乐部

● The cricket club built in the Race Course

● 跑马场观赛看台

● The stand of the Race Course for watching the matches

● 新世界游乐场屋顶花园上的观赛人群

● The spectators on the roof garden of the New World pleasure ground

● 早期的赛马活动

● Horse racing activities in the early time

● 早期的赛马活动

● Horse racing activities in the early time

五

南京路 Nanjing Road

● 跑马场西藏路一侧

● One side of the racecourse near Xizang Road

● 20世纪30年代的赛马实况

● The scene of horse racing in the 1930s

● 跑马场每年春秋两季举行跑马大赛，1909 年以后才允许中国人购票观赛

● There are two horse racing matches in spring and autumn every year held in the racecourse. After 1909, Chinese were permitted to buy tickets and watch the matches

● 观看跑马大赛的人们

● Peopie watching The racing matches

五

南京路 Nanjing Road

大清朱家角郵局

1926 年华安大厦建成，是当时中国人造的最高建筑，1939 年更名金门饭店

Hua'an building which was the highest building in China that time was completed in 1926 and renamed Golden Gate Hotel in 1939

1934 年建成 83.8 米高的国际饭店，在近半个世纪中该楼为上海第一高楼

The International Hotel was completed in 1934 with a height of 83.8 meters which was the highest building in Shanghai nearly half a century

1933 年重建的跑马总会大楼和大光明大戏院

The reconstructed building of the Race Club and the Grand Theatre in 1933

跑马总会大楼曾为上海博物馆和图书馆，1997 年改为上海美术馆

The building of the Race Club was once Shanghai Museum and Shanghai Library and it was changed to Shanghai Art Museum in 1997

20 世纪 30 年代跑马场全景

A full view of the race course in the 1930s

1951 年跑马场改建为人民公园和人民广场

The race course was rebuilt and became People's Park and People's Square in 1951

● 在人民公园划船的游客

● Tourists were rowing in People's Park

● 金门饭店 1958 年改为华侨饭店，现恢复原名

● Golden Gate Hotel was changed to Overseas Chinese Hotel in 1958 and now it has resumed the former name

20世纪70年代的人民公园

People's Park in the 1970s

20世纪80年代的人民公园

People's Park in the 1980s

20世纪50年代的人民广场

People's Square in the 1950s

1958年人民广场上举行“五一”节游行

The May Day parade in People's Square in 1958

20 世纪 60 年代的人民广场

People's Square in the 1960s

20 世纪 70 年代的人民广场

People's Square in the 1970s

20 世纪 90 年代建设中的人民广场

People's Square under construction in the 1990s

20 世纪 90 年代的人民广场

People's Square in the 1990s

1995 年市政府大厦建成使用

Shanghai Government Building was completed and put into service in 1995

1996 年建成的上海博物馆

Shanghai Museum was completed in 1996

1998 年建成的上海大剧院

Shanghai Grand Theater was completed in 1998

1999 年建成的上海城市规划展示馆

Shanghai Urban Planning Exhibition Center was completed in 1999

人民广场上的飞鸽

The flying pigeons in People's Square

人民广场上的音乐喷水池

The Music Fountain in People's Square

21 世纪初的人民广场

People's Square in the 2000s

人民广场全景

A full view of People's Square

静安寺于1216年迁至现址，为上海著名古刹

Jing'an Temple moved to its current site in 1216 which is a famous ancient temple in Shanghai

1863年筑成由跑马场通往静安寺的马路

The road from the race course to Jing'an Temple was completed in 1863

南京西路原名静安寺路，早期因静安寺前有一口泉井而取名涌泉路

West Nanjing Road was originally called Jing'An Temple Road. In early times, it was called Bubbling Well Road because of the artesian well in front of it

静安寺前的泉井

The artesian well in front of Jing'An Temple

五

南京路 Nanjing Road

20 世纪 30 年代静安寺前旧景

The old scene in front of Jing'an Temple in the 1930s

20 世纪 30 年代静安寺前旧景

The old scene in front of Jing'an Temple in the 1930s

20 世纪 50 年代的静安寺

Jing'an Temple in the 1950s

21 世纪初的静安寺

Jing'an Temple in the 2000s

五
南京路 Nangjing Road

静安寺路旁的河浜

The streamlet at the roadside of Jing'An Temple Road

1908 年静安寺路开通有轨电车

The streetcar was opened on Jing'an Temple Road in 1908

20 世纪初的静安寺路

Jing'an Temple Road in the 1900s

20 世纪 10 年代的静安寺路

Jing'an Temple Road in the 1910s

五

南京路 Nangjing Road

20 世纪初的静安寺路东段

The east part of Jing'an Temple Road in the 1900s

21 世纪初的南京西路东段

The east part of West Nanjing Road in the 2000s

- 20世纪30年代的国际饭店
- The International Hotel in the 1930s

- 20世纪80年代的国际饭店
- The International Hotel in the 1980s

五

南京路 Nanjing Road

● 建于1903年的意大利领事馆，位于今南京西路成都路口，已拆除

● Italian Consulate built in 1930 was located at the intersection of current West Nanjing Road and Chengdu Road which has been demolished now

● 建于1879年的斜桥总会为英国侨民俱乐部

● The Country club built in 1879 was a club for English emigrants

- 斜桥总会位于南京西路青海路，1974 年在该址建上海电视塔
- The Country club was located on West Nanjing Road and Qinhai Road where Shanghai TV Tower was built in 1974

- 2002 年改建为广电大厦
- It was rebuilt as Shanghai TV Centre in 2002

五

南京路 Nanjing Road

1928 年建成德义大楼，位于今南京西路石门二路口

Deyi Building located on current West Nanjing Road and Shimen No.2 Rd was built in 1928

德义大楼 1958 年开设少年儿童书店

A bookstore for youths and children was opened in Deyi Building in 1958

静安寺路街景

The street scene on Jing'an Temple Road

静安寺路街景

The street scene on Jing'an Temple Road

五

南京路 Nanjing Road

辛家花园建于南京西路以北泰兴路一带，1914 年至 1921 年康有为在此园居住

Xinjia Garden was built near Taixing Road at the north side of West Nanjing Road. Kang Youwei lived here from 1914 to 1921

建于 1882 年的张园，位于今茂名北路泰兴路之间，20 世纪 20 年代渐废

Zhang Garden built in 1882 was located between today's North Maoming Road and Taixing Road which lay waste in the 1920s.

● 大华饭店1922年由麦边花园改建而成，1927年蒋介石与宋美龄在此举行婚礼

● Dahua Hotel was converted from Maibian Garden in 1922. The wedding ceremony of Chiang Kai-shek and Sung Mei-ling was held there in 1927

● 大华饭店于1929年烧毁，1941年在旧址上建美琪大剧院

● Dahua Hotel was burnt down in 1929 and the old site was built as Shanghai Majestic Theatre in 1941

愚园建于1890年，位于今愚园路常德路一带，20世纪20年代渐废

Yu Garden near today's Yu Yuan Road and Changde Road was built in 1890 which lay waste in the 1920s

愚园旧景

The old scene of Yu garden

愚园内的茶室

The tea room in Yu Garden

愚园内的亭阁

The pavilion in Yu Garden

五

南京路 Nanjing Road

- 1945 年静安寺路更名为南京西路
- Jing'an Temple Road was renamed as West Nanjing Road in 1945

- 20 世纪 60 年代的南京西路
- West Nanjing Road in the 1960s

5

南京路

Nangjing Road

20世纪80年代的南京西路

West Nanjing Road in the 1980s

五
南京路 Nangjing Road
大清朱家角邨局

1932 年在静安寺西北建成百乐门舞厅，1954 年改为红都影剧场

Paramount Hall was built on the northwest side of Jing'an Temple in 1932 which was changed to Red Centre cinema in 1954

2002 年修缮后恢复原名的百乐门

After reconstruction in 2002 it resumed the former name Paramount Hall

21世纪初的南京西路夜景

The night scene of West Nanjing Road in the 2000s

南京西路静安公园

Jing'an Park on West Nanjing Road

21 世纪初的南京西路

West Nanjing Road in the 2000s

南京西路上高楼林立

Clusters of highrises on west Nanjing Road

Carte postale
Union postale
收回租界紀念
成獨立自主
十二年八月一日
上海
中国人民邮政
明信片
上海外白渡桥
CARD.

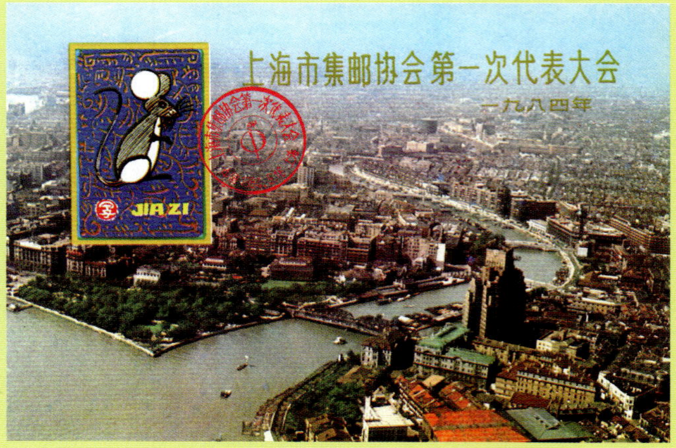

19 世纪的外滩，大上海由这里起步

The Bund in the 19th century—Shanghai Stemming From Here

美好城市的百年变迁

——明信片上看上海

The Centennial Changes of the Dynamic City

Seeing Shanghai From the Postcards

【下册】 Vol. II

姚丽旋　编著

Compiled by Yao Lixuan

上海大学出版社

Shanghai University Press

POST CARD.
大清朱家角郵局
CHINESE IMPERIAL POST
FOUR CENTS
POST

六

淮　海　路

Huaihai Road

1950年为纪念淮海战役而命名的淮海路，东起人民路，西至凯旋路，全长约7公里，分为淮海东路、淮海中路和淮海西路。早期的公馆马路为法租界的繁华之地，自1900年开始，法租界经过三次越界筑路形成了现在的淮海路格局。淮海路曾经六易其名，多少带有战争及政权更迭的色彩。如今，淮海路作为上海的特色商业街，融东西方文化为一体，成为时尚的代名词；而淮海路一带保存的革命遗迹，正是人们领略历史文化最佳的人文景观。

Huaihai Road which starts from Renmin Road in the east and ends at Kaixuan Road in the west is a seven-kilometer-long street named in honor of Huai-Hai Campaign in 1950 and it is divided into East, Middle and West Huaihai Road. The early Rue Du Consulat was a flourishing place. From 1900, the French Concession paved the roads beyond the mark for three times and made today's structure of Huaihai Road. Huaihai Road has changed its name for six times which was permeated with the color of wars and alternation of governments. Today, as a special commercial street in Shanghai, Huaihai Road has become the synonymy of fashion blending the culture of East and West. The revolutionary remains which were preserved there are the best human landscape for people to appreciate history and culture.

六

淮海路 Huaihai Road

1917 年上海法国新租界分图

Detail drawing of French New Concession in Shanghai in 1917

法国领事馆于 1854 年迁至外滩，位于公馆马路口，1987 年被拆除

The French Consulate was moved to the bund in 1854 located at the crossing of Rue Du Consulat. It was removed in 1987

19 世纪后叶，公馆马路为法租界的中心街区

In the late 19th century, Rue Du Consulat became the main street in the French Concession

公馆马路上的人力车

Rickshaws on Rue Du Consulat

六

淮海路 Huaihai Road

20世纪初的公馆马路街景

The street scene of Rue Du Consulat in the 1900s

20世纪初的公馆马路街景

The street scene of Rue Du Consulat in the 1900s

● 公馆马路也称法租界大马路，1943 年更名为金陵路

● Rue Du Consulat was renamed as Jinling Road in 1943

六

淮海路 Huaihai Road

● 建于1865年的法租界公董局大楼，1929年被拆除

● The Municipal building of the French Concession built in 1865 was demolished in 1929

● 早年的法租界西式旅馆，旧址位于今金陵东路四川南路口

● Early western-style hotel of the French Concession. The old site was located on the intersection of today's East Jinling Road and South Sichuan Road

民国时期的公馆马路

Rue Du Consulat in the period of the Republic of China

1913 年迁至新址的中法学堂，位于今淮海东路，1951 年更名为光明中学

Sino–French School was moved to its new place on Huaihai Road in 1913 and changed its name to Guangming Middle School in 1951

1901 年建成的宝昌路，1915 年以法国霞飞元帅之名命名为霞飞路

Baochang Road was built in 1901 and in 1915 it was renamed as Xiafei Road after the French marshal Xia fei

20 世纪 20 年代的霞飞路

Xiafei Road in the 1920s

● 建于1921年的恩派亚大戏院，1956年改名为嵩山电影院，已拆除

● Empire Theatre built in 1921 was renamed as Songshan Cinema in 1956 which has been demolished now

● 今淮海中路上的东风中学，为昔日法租界巡捕房之一

● Dongfeng Middle School on Middle Huaihai Road was one of the former police stations in the French Concession

六 淮海路 Huaihai Road

● 1929 年公董局迁至霞飞路，1958 年为比乐中学校舍

● The Municipal building was moved to Xiafei Road in 1929 and became the school house of Bile Middle School in 1958

● 20 世纪 90 年代改建为中环广场

● In the 1990s it is rebuilt as Central Plaza

淮海路远眺

A distant view of Huaihai Road

1924年建于霞飞路的尚贤坊石库门里弄住宅

Shangxianfang Shikumen built in 1924 on Xiafei Road

● 兴业路上这幢石库门民居，是中国共产党的诞生地，1921年7月23日中共“一大”在此召开

● This folk house on Xingye Road was the birthplace of the Communist Party and the First National Congress of the Communist Party was held here on July 23rd, 1921

● 中共“一大”会议纪念馆，该地区现为新天地景区

● Commemorative Museum of the First National Congress of the Communist Party. Now it is the scenic area of Xintiandi

新天地始建于1999年

Xintiandi built in 1999

新天地夜景

The night scene of Xintiandi

六

淮海路 Huaihai Road

大清朱家角邮局

新天地东侧的太平桥园区

Taipingqiao garden on the east side of Xintiandi

太平桥全景

A full view of Taipingqiao

● 培恩公寓建于1930年，1956年在此开设上海妇女用品商店

● Payne Apartments was built in 1930 and in 1956 Shanghai Women Goods Store was opened there

● 淮海路旧景

● An old scene of Huaihai Road

六

淮海路 Huaihai Road

● 20 世纪 30 年代的巴黎大戏院，现为淮海电影院

● Paris theatre in the 1930s and now it is Huaihai Cinema

● 21 世纪初的时代广场

● Time Square in the 2000s

瑞金宾馆

Ruijin hotel

● 建于1917年的英商住宅，今为瑞金宾馆

● The apartment of the English businessmen built in 1917 is Ruijin Hotel today

科学会堂

The college Municipal Francais

● 创办于1904年的法国总会，今为上海科学会堂

● The French Club was founded in 1904. Now it is Shanghai Science Hall

六

淮海路 Huaihai Road

1909年由法军军营改建的顾家宅公园

Gujiazhai Park was converted from the French military camp in 1909

顾家宅公园俗称法国公园，1943年改称为复兴公园

Gujiazhai Park known as the French Park was renamed as Fuxing Park in 1943

20 世纪 50 年代的复兴公园

Fuxing Park in the 1950s

21 世纪初的复兴公园

Fuxing Park in the 2000s

六 淮海路 Huaihai Road

● 位于香山路上的孙中山故居，是孙中山和夫人宋庆龄1918年至1924年在上海的寓所

● Residence of Dr. Sun Yat-sen, located on Xiangshan Road, was the apartment of Dr. Sun Yat-sen and his wife Madame Soong Qingling in Shanghai from 1918 to 1924

● 思南路上的周恩来公馆为1946年国共谈判期间中共代表团驻沪办事处

● Zhou Residence located on Sinan Road was the Shanghai representative office of the Communist Party of China during the negotiation period between Kuomingtang and the Communist Party in 1946

毛泽东1924年在茂名北路的寓所

The apartment of Chairman Mao on North Maoming Road in 1924

1920年8月上海社会主义青年团在渔阳里创立

Shanghai Socialist Youth League was founded at Yuyangli in August, 1920

六

淮海路 Huaihai Road

● 1932 年建成的国泰大戏院

● Cathay Theatre built in 1932

● 1954 年更名为国泰电影院

● It was renamed as Cathay Cinema in 1954

1929年建成的华懋公寓，位于今茂名南路

Cathay Mansion, located on today's South Maoming Road was built in 1929

华懋公寓南侧

The south side of Cathay Mansion

六

淮海路 Huaihai Road

● 华懋公寓1951年改为锦江饭店，曾是新中国上海的第一国宾馆

● Cathay Mansion was changed to Jinjiang Hotel in 1951 which was the first state guesthouse of new China in Shanghai

● 1934年建成峻岭公寓，俗称“十八层楼”，现为锦江饭店中楼

● Junling apartment, built in 1934 which was called the Eighteen-storey Building is now the middle building of Jinjiang Hotel

● 1989年建成153米高的新锦江大酒店，为当时上海高楼之冠

● The new Jinjiang Hotel with a length of 153 meters was built in 1989 which ranked first in the tall buildings in Shanghai that time

● 中间建筑为建于1959年的锦江小礼堂，1972年“中美上海公报”在这里诞生

● The middle building was the small hall of Jinjiang Hotel built in 1959 in which Sino-American Shanghai Communique was born in 1972

1926 年在原德人乡村俱乐部旧址重建的法国总会

The site of the former German country club was rebuilt as French Chamber in 1926

1953 年改为市政协文化俱乐部，1960 年划归锦江饭店

In 1953 it was renamed as the cultural club of Shanghai Political Consultative Conference and in 1960 it was incorporated into Jinjiang Hotel

1990年建成花园饭店，原法国总会建筑成为花园饭店的裙楼

Garden Hotel was built in 1990 and the building of the former French Chamber became its annex

21世纪初的锦江饭店和花园饭店

Jingjiang Hotel and Garden hotel in the 2000s

六

淮海路 Huaihai Road

20世纪30年代的霞飞路与迈尔西爱路口

The intersection of Xiafei Road and Route Cardinal Mercier in the 1930s

21世纪初的淮海中路与茂名南路口

The intersection of middle Huaihai Road and South Maoming Road in the 2000s

- 淮海中路大方公寓
- Dafang apartment on Middle Huaihai Road

- 20 世纪 90 年代的淮海中路夜景
- The night view of Middle Huaihai Road in the 1990s

六

淮海路 Huaihai Road

● 位于淮海中路陕西南路口的巴黎春天百货大楼

● Printemps located between middle Huaihai Road and south Shanxi Road

● 建于1928年的逸园跑狗场，位于今陕西南路永嘉路处

● Yiyuan dog race ring built in 1928 is now located between south Shanxi Road and Yongjia Road

● 1953年跑狗场改建为文化广场，曾为上海市文艺演出和政治集会的主要场所

● In 1953 it was rebuilt as a cultural square which was a main venue for theatrical performances and political meetings of Shanghai

● 建于1927年的霞飞路淮海坊住宅

● Huaihai Fang residence on Xiafei Road built in 1927

● 建于1938年的上方花园，为公寓式花园里弄

● Shangfang Garden built in 1938 is an apartment—style garden lane

建于1931年的恩派亚公寓，今为淮海大楼

Empire Mansion built in 1931 is called Huaihai building today

建于1924年的诺曼底公寓，今为武康大楼

Normandy Apartments built in 1924 is called Wukang building today

六

淮海路 Huaihai Road

● 建于1996年的上海图书馆

● Shanghai Library built in 1996

● 宋庆龄故居，中华人民共和国名誉主席宋庆龄曾在此居住30多年

● The former residence of Madame. Soong Qingling, the Honorary President of the People' s Republic of China, in which she had lived for more than 30 years

● 创办于1896年的南洋公学，1921年改称为上海交通大学

● Nanyang College opened in 1896 was changed to Shanghai Jiao Tong University in 1921

● 建于1935年的学校正门，1937年学校迁至重庆，校址被日本东亚同文书院占用

● The portal of the university was built in 1935. It moved to Chongqing in 1937 and this site was occupied by Japan East Asia Common Culture College

六 淮海路 Huaihai Road

● 建于1900年的上院大学部

● The College division built in 1900

● 1954年改建后的新上院

● New Shangyuan rebuilt in 1954

- 建于 1918 年的学校图书馆
- The library built in 1918

- 今华山路上的上海交通大学正门
- The portal of Shanghai Jiao Tong University on today's Huashan Road

六

淮海路 Huaihai Road

● 1992年淮海路进行大改造，一批商务楼宇建成

● There was a big scale reconstruction on Huaihai Road in 1992 and many commercial buildings were erected

楼峰街谷
Crest of the building and vista

21 世纪初的淮海路

Huaihai Road in the 2000s

21 世纪初的淮海路

Huaihai Road in the 2000s

六

淮海路 Huaihai Road

● 淮海路店面夜景

● The night scene of the storefronts on Huaihai Road

● 淮海路店面夜景

● The night scene of the storefronts on Huaihai Road

淮海路街景夜色

Streetscape and night view on Huaihai Road

六

淮海路 Huaihai Road

淮海路现代建筑群

Modern architectural complex on Huaihai Road

七

四　川　路

Sichuan Road

No. 162. North Sze Chuen Road Near The Rifle Butt Shanghai.

四川路由四川南路、四川中路、四川北路组成，全长5.3公里，而地处虹口区的四川北路是上海三大商业名街之一。四川路1865年始建于英租界，通过苏州河上的四川路桥与美租界相接。租界当局以修建靶子场为由，非法越界筑路，将四川路不断向北延伸。如果说南京路的扩展与“跑马”有关，那么四川路的历史可以说与“枪声”密切相关。20世纪30年代，这里成为两次淞沪战争的发源地，同时也绘就了军民抗战的壮丽画卷。百年前虹口商业中心由百老汇路、吴淞路向四川路转移，如今面向21世纪，四川路将传承历史文化打造出自己的特色街景。

Sichuan Road includes South Sichuan Road, Middle Sichuan Road and North Sichuan Road with a total length of 5.3 kilometers. North Sichuan Road located in Hongkou District is one of the three famous commercial streets in Shanghai. Sichuan Road was first built in the British Concession in 1865 connecting with the American Concession by Suzhou River on Sichuan Road Bridge. The authorities of the Concession paved road beyond the mark illegally on the grounds of constructing shooting range and extended Sichuan Road northward. If we say the extension of Nanjing Road was related to the horse race, the history of Sichuan Road was closely related to the war. In the 1930s, Sichuan Road was the cradle land of the two Songhu Battles describing the splendid handscroll of painting that soldiers and civilians fought the invaders. One hundred years ago, Hongkou commercial center was shifted from Broadway Road and Wusong Road to Sichuan Road, and now, toward the 21st century, Sichuan Road will create a character of its own by passing down the history and culture.

七

四川路 Sichuan Road

大清朱家角邮局

1917 年上海美租界分图，英美租界于 1899 年改称为"公共租界"

This is the detail drawing of American Settlement in Shanghai in 1917. The British Concession and the American Concession were renamed as International Settlement in 1899

虹口，因虹口港河流而得名

Hongkou District was named after Hongkou Creek

虹口港黄浦江入口

The entrance of Hongkou Creek to Huangpu River

建于19世纪60年代的百老汇路

Broadway Road built in the 1860s

七 四川路 Sichuan Road

● 20 世纪初的百老汇路街景，1943 年改称大名路

● The street scene of Broadway Road in the 1900s which was renamed as Da Ming Road in 1943

● 百老汇路街景

● The street scene of Broadway Road

● 北望百老汇路，右侧为香港上海支行和礼查饭店

● Looking northward into Broadway Road, we see Bank of Hongkong, Shanghai Sub-Branch and Astor House Hotel on the right side

● 外白渡桥北堍，左侧为建于1906年的英商电车公司

● Looking northward from Waibaidu Bridge, we see Shanghai Electric Construction Co. Ltd built in 1906 on the left side

七 四川路 Sichuan Road

百老汇路和黄浦路口

The intersection of Broadway Road and Huangpu Road

早期的黄浦路

The early Huangpu Road

- 黄浦路上的教堂
- Church on Huangpu Road

- 黄浦路上的德国领事馆和教堂
- Germany Consulate and Church on Huangpu Road

七

四川路 Sichuan Road

大清朱家角邮局

● 建于1931年的中国企业银行大楼和建于1943年的会德丰大楼，位于今延安东路四川中路口

● The building of Chinese Corporate Bank built in 1931 and Huidefeng Building built in 1943 are located on the intersection of today's East Yan'an Road and Middle Sichuan Road

● 建于1910年的永年人寿保险公司，位于今广东路四川中路口

● Yongnian Life Insurance Company built in 1910 was located on the intersection of Guangdong Road and Middle Sichuan Road

● 建于1905年的德国邮政局，位于今福州路四川中路口

● German post office built in 1905 was located on the intersection of today's Fuzhou Road and Middle Sichuan Road

● 1903年建于四川路的日本三井物业公司上海分店

● Shanghai branch of Japanese Sanjing Property Management Company built on Sichuan Road in 1903

七 四川路 Sichuan Road

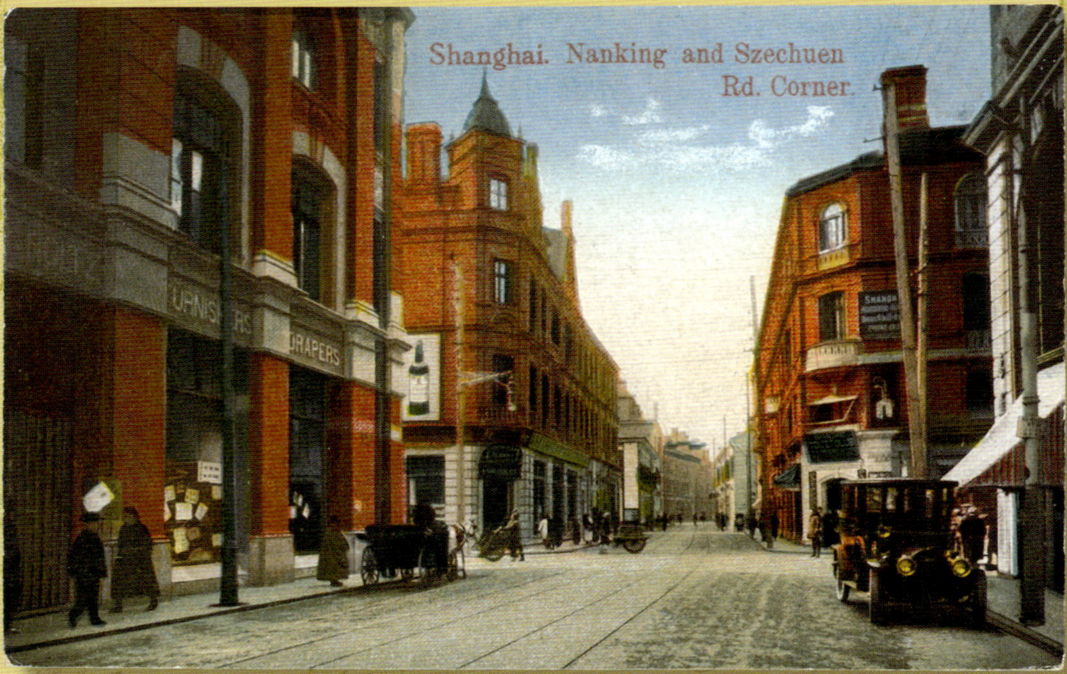

● 20 世纪 10 年代的南京路四川路口

● Nanjing Road at the intersection of Sichuan Road in the 1910s

● 20 世纪 20 年代的四川路桥南堍

● The south side of Sichuan Road Bridge in the 1920s

7 四川路 Sichuan Road

● 1924 年建于四川路桥北堍的上海邮政大楼

● Shanghai Postal Building built on the north side of Sichuan Road Bridge in 1924

● 2006 年上海邮政博物馆在此开馆

● Shanghai Postal Museum opened here in 2006

七 四川路 Sichuan Road

- 建于1934年的新亚大酒店，1937年在此成立汪伪上海市大道政府
- New Aisa Hotel was built in 1934. In 1937 Wang Jingwei puppet regime called Shanghai Dadao Municipal Government was established here

- 1945年北四川路更名为四川北路
- North Sichuan Road was renamed as Sichuan North Road in 1945

● 早期的天潼路

● The early Tiantong Road

● 1915 年建于百老汇路上的日本电信局，已拆除

● Japanese Telegraph Exchange office was built on Broadway Road in 1915 which was removed now

七

四川路 Sichuan Road

大清朱家角邮局

● 20世纪初的武昌路

● Wuchuang Road in the 1900s

● 早期的长治路街景

● The street scene of Changzhi Road

● 1884 年迁至南浔路的圣芳济学院，今北虹中学

● St. Francis Xavier's College was moved to Nanxun Road in 1884. (Today's Beihong Middle School)

● 1914 年在文监师路上建立的日本俱乐部，已拆除

● Japanese club was built on W.J. Boone Road in 1914 which was removed now

七

四川路 Sichuan Road

- 早期的塘沽路
- The early Tanggu Road

- 1860年以后在塘沽路一带形成菜市
- A market was formed in the region of Tanggu Road after 1860

1891 年建立木结构的三角地菜场

The wood structural triangle market was built in 1891

早期的三角地菜场

The early triangle market

七

四川路 Sichuan Road

● 1923 年三角地菜场改建为水泥结构建筑

● Triangle market was rebuilt into a cement structure building in 1923

● 三角地菜场是上海最早和规模最大的室内菜场

● Triangle market was the earliest and largest indoor market in Shanghai

● 早期的菜市街　今为马厂路

● The early Market Street (today's Machang Road)

7 四川路 Sichuan Road

● 1895 年建于昆山路的昆山花园

● Kunshan Garden built on Kunshan Road in 1895

七

四川路 Sichuan Road

● 昆山花园是上海最早的儿童花园

● Kunshan Garden is the earliest children's garden in Shanghai

● 昆山花园内景

● The interior of Kunshan Garden

1876 年在乍浦路创办的日本佛教东本愿寺上海别院

Shanghai Branch of Japanese Buddhist Temple called Dongbenyuan Temple was established on Zhapu Road in 1876

早期的昆山路和吴淞路路口

The intersection of Kunshan Road and Wusong Road in early times

七 四川路 Sichuan Road

1856 年填浜筑路建成的广东街，1863 年更名为吴淞路

The creek was filled to pave road and built as Guangdong Street in 1856 which was renamed as Wusong Road in 1863

吴淞路为日本风格的商业街

Wusong Road was a Japanese style shopping street

工部局屠牛場（上海）

A newly constructed abbatoir at Hongkew, Shanghai.

上海虹口に最新に建設せられたる屠牛場なり。

● 1894 年设虹口宰牲场，此为建于 1933 年的工部局宰牲场

● Hongkou Abattoir was built in 1894 and this was the abattoir of the Municipal Council in 1933

上　海　神　社

上海神社は上海全居留民の氏神なり
新公園の南方に鎮座す

● 1933 年建于江湾路的日本上海神社

● Japanese shrine in Shanghai on Jiangwan Road in 1933

七

四川路 Sichuan Road

1867年上海工部局在吴淞路建"沈家湾救火会"，该救火会也称虹口消防区队

Shanghai Municipal Council set up Shen Jiawan Fire Station on Wusong Road in 1867 which was also called Hongkou Fire Station

消防队

Fire Station

● 正在进行演练的消防队

● Members of the Fire Station were drilling

七

四川路 Sichuan Road

20世纪初的四川路横浜桥

Hengbang Bridge on Sichuan Road in the 1900s

20世纪初的北四川路已成为繁华的商业街道

North Sichuan Road became a busy shopping street in the 1900s

● 北四川路街景

● The street scene of North Sichuan Road

● 四川路上的有轨电车

● Street cars on Sichuan Road

七 四川路 Sichuan Road

大清朱家角郵局

四川路周聚康四书社印行

Zhou Jukang Four Books Press on Sichuan Road

四川路上的商店

The stores on Sichuan Road

早期的老靶子路，今为武进路

The early Range Road (today's Wujin Road)

20世纪20年代的北四川路老靶子路口，今为武进路口

The intersection of the Range Road and North Sichuan Road in the 1920s (today's intersection of Wujin Road)

七

四川路 Sichuan Road

20 世纪 30 年代的北四川路

North Sichuan Road in the 1930s

因日本人多聚居虹口一带，北四川路上日本商行林立

Because many Japanese lived in the region of Hongkou District, there were many Japanese commercial firms on North Sichuan Road

1907 年于北四川路建日本小学，1946 年改为上海市博物馆，今为虹口区实验中学

The Japanese primary school was built on North Sichuan Road in 1907 which was rebuilt into Shanghai Museum in 1946 and now it is Hongkou Experimental Middle School

雨后的北四川路街道

The street of North Sichuan Road after a rain

七 四川路 Sichuan Road

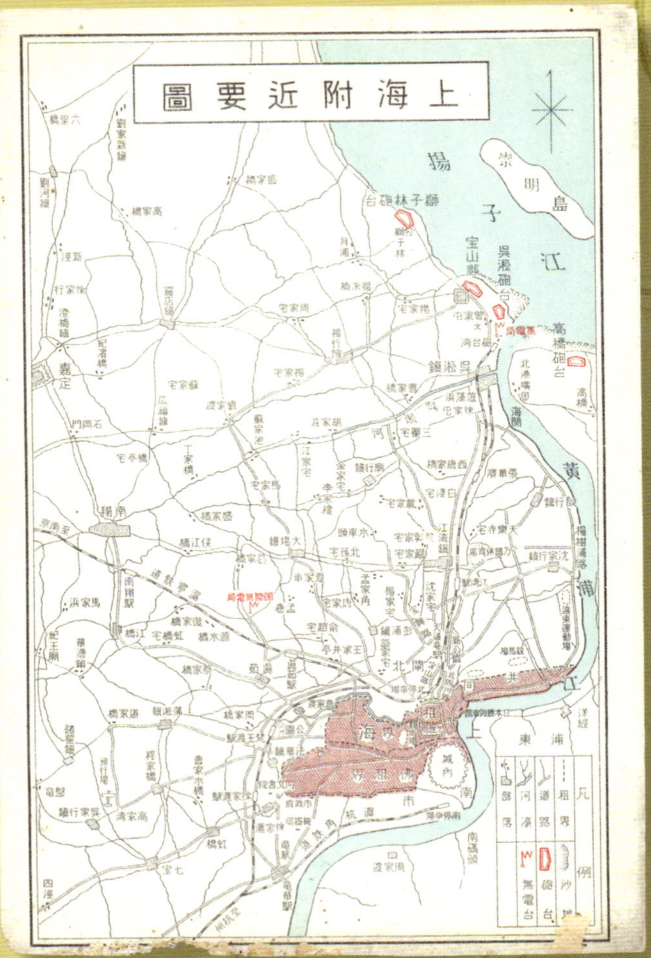

- 在淞沪战争中北四川路成为军事要道
- North Sichuan Road became martial artery in Song — Hu Campaign

- 天通庵车站和八字桥成为当年激战之地
- Tiantongan Bus Station and the splayed bridge became places of fierce battles that time

7

Sichuan Road

四川路

Peissuchuanlo Road, Shanghai （上海）日本陸戰隊警備下之北四川路

- 被日军侵占的北四川路
- The North Sichuan Road which was invaded by the Japanese trcops

北四川路アイシス附近の警備 Landing force in the near of Isis Theatre

- 被日军侵占的北四川路
- The North Sichuan Road which was invaded by the Japanese troops

七 四川路 Sichuan Road

● 日军在北四川路构筑街垒

● The Japanese army built street barricade on North Sichuan Road

● 北四川路附近逃难的人群

● The refugees around North Sichuan Road

● 1929年迁至北四川路的内山书店

● Neishan bookstore was moved to North Sichuan Road in 1929

● 20世纪40年代北四川路夜景

● The night scene of North Sichuan Road in the 1940s

七
四川路
Sichuan Road

1893 年建于北四川路的工部局西童男校

Public School for Boys of the Municipal Committee built on the North Sichuan Road in 1893

1904 年西童男校改称汉壁礼西童学校

Public School for Boys was renamed as Thomas Hanbary School for Boys in 1904

1946 年汉壁礼西童学校更名为复兴中学，今为民办新复兴初级中学

Thomas Hanbary School for Boys was renamed as Fuxing Middle School in 1946 and now it is the new private Fuxing Junior Middle School

建于 1998 年的复兴高级中学

Fuxing High School built in 1998

七

四川路 Sichuan Road

● 建在江湾路的日本海军陆战队司令部

● Japanese Navel Landing Party's Headquarters built on Jiangwan Road

● 1924 年改建为日本海军特别陆战队大楼，是侵沪日军的最高指挥部

● It was rebuilt into the building of Japanese Special Navel Landing Party in 1924 which was the high command of the Japanese troops against Shanghai

日军装甲车库

Vehicle hangar of the Japanese army

六三花园是 1912 年建于江湾路的一座日式花园

Liusan Garden was a Japanese style garden built on Jiangwan Road in 1912

七

四川路 Sichuan Road

大清朱家角郵局

六三花园毁于1932年的战火，今花园路由此得名

Liusan Garden was destroyed in the war-flame in 1932 and hence today's Garden Road

毁于战火的六三花园

Liusan Garden was destroyed in the war-flame

建于1905年的新靶子场公园，1922年更名为虹口公园

The New Range Park was built in 1905 and renamed as Hongkou Park in 1922

虹口公园曾为日本人俱乐部附属园

Hongkou Park was once the Japanese club garden

七

四川路 Sichuan Road

1945年改称中正公园，解放后又复名为虹口公园

In 1945 it was renamed as Zhongzheng Park and resumed the name Hongkou Park after Liberation

虹口公园旧景

The old scene of Hongkou Park

1936 年建于万国公墓的鲁迅墓

The tomb of Lu Xun was built Wanguo Cemetery in 1936

1956 年鲁迅墓由万国公墓移入虹口公园

The tomb of Lu Xun was moved to Hongkou Park in 1956

20 世纪 50 年代的虹口公园

Hongkou Park in the 1950s

20 世纪 60 年代的鲁迅墓，1988 年虹口公园更名为鲁迅公园

The tomb of Lu Xun in the 1960s, Hongkou Park was renamed as Luxun Park in 1988

建于1999年的上海鲁迅纪念馆

Shanghai LuXun Memorial Hall built in 1999

位于山阴路的鲁迅故居

Former Residence of Lu Xun built on Shanyin Road

七 四川路 Sichuan Road

● 位于四川北路北端的多伦路

● Duolun Road located on the north side of North Sichuan Road

● 1998 年多伦路建为文化名人街

● Duolun Road was built as a cultural street in 1998

● 建于1928年的鸿德堂，该教堂采用中国式斗拱飞檐结构

● Hongde Church was built in 1928 with a Chinese temple style

● 1930年中国左翼作家联盟成立纪念馆

● Commemorative museum of China League of Left-Wing Writers established in 1930

七

四川路 Sichuan Road

建于1951年的虹口体育场

Hongkou stadium built in 1951

1999年改建为虹口足球场

Hongkou stadium was rebuilt and became Hongkou Soccer Stadium in 1999

20 世纪 90 年代的四川北路商业街

The shopping street on North Sichuan Road in the 1990s

21 世纪初的多伦路街景

The street scene of Duolun Road in the 2000s

七 四川路 Sichuan Road 大清朱家角邮局

四川北路夜景

The night scene of North Sichuan Road

21 世纪初的四川北路绿地公园

Green Park on North Sichuan Road in the 2000s

八

其他街区

Other Blocks

南京路、淮海路、四川路是上海负有盛名的三大街，仅有三大名街还不能尽显上海城市街区的风貌。今河南中路，旧时称界路，是英租界筑成的早期道路。界路两侧的街道纵横有序，被称为棋盘街。虽然棋盘街的地名早已消失，但它构成了近代城市街区发展的原型。随着时代的变迁和城市化的推进，上海街区建设不断扩展，日新月异。由于历史上产生的上海其他街区的明信片很有限，本章展示的河南路、福州路、江西路、西藏路、杨树浦路以及徐家汇、江湾五角场等街区的明信片，仅从一个侧面来印证上海街区所发生的变化。

Nanjing Road, Huaihai Road and Sichuan Road are three well-known streets in Shanghai. However, the three roads cannot utterly show the style and features of the city blocks in Shanghai. Today's Middle Henan Road, once called Boundary Road, is the early road built by the British Concession. Because the streets on both sides of the Boundary Road are arranged in perfect order, it is called Chessboard Street. Though the name of Chessboard Street has gone, it forms the original shape of the block development of the city in modern times. With the changing of the times and the pulsion of urbanization, the constructions of the city blocks in Shanghai keep expanding. Due to the limited number of the post cards on other city blocks in Shanghai's history, this chapter only reflects the change of the city blocks from one aspect with the show of the post cards on Henna Road, Fuzhou Road, Jiangxi Road, Xizang Road, Yangshupu Road, Xujiahui and Jiangwan Wu Jiao Chang, etc.

河南路是1848年英租界第一次扩张前形成的一条界路

Henan Road was a boundary road formed before the first expansion of the British Concession in 1848

河南路街景

The street scene of Henan Road

● 清末河南路街景

● The street scene of Henan Road in the late Qing Dynasty

八

其他街区 Other Blocks

大清朱家角郵局

● 1865 年福州路被命名，俗称四马路，在清末是上海最繁华的商业街

● Fuzhou Road, named in 1865 and commonly referred to as Fourth Avenue, was the busiest shopping street in the late Qing Dynasty

● 福州路上的青莲阁为清代上海著名的茶楼

● Qingliange on Fuzhou Road was a famous teahouse in Shanghai in Qing Dynasty

● 青莲阁茶楼，是上海最早放映无声电影
●场所，现址为外文书店

● Qingliange tea house was the earliest place that projected silent films in Shanghai and now the site is foreign language bookstore

八 其他街区 Other Blocks

- 福州路上的中央巡捕房和五洲大药房
- The Central Police Station and Wuzhou Drug Store on Fuzhou Road

- 福州路上的一层楼
- Yi Cenglou on Fuzhou Road

● 福州路上的五层茶楼和沪江第一楼

● The No.1 Tea House of Shanghai and the five-storey teahouse on Fuzhou Road

● 福州路上的中西大药房

● The Great China Dispensary on Fuzhou Road

● 福州路上的东方第一游戏园

● The First Eastern Game Zone on Fuzhou Road

● 福州路上集中了大量的出版机构和文化用品商店

● Fuzhou Road gathered many presses and cultural goods shops

● 福州路素有“文化街”之称

● Fuzhou Road has enjoyed the name of “cultural street”

八 其他街区 Other Blocks

● 申报1872年创办于望平街

● Shanghai Journal was founded on Wangping Street in 1872

● 图中塔型建筑为1904年创办的时报馆

● The tower shape building was the times newspaper office founded in 1904

20 世纪 30 年代的福州路街景

The street scene of Fuzhou Road in the 1930s

20 世纪 30 年代的福州路街景

The street scene of Fuzhou Road in the 1930s

八 其他街区 Other Blocks

1927 年的杏花楼酒家，为当时上海最大的粤菜馆

1927's Xinghualou restaurant was the largest Cantonese Restaurant that time in Shanghai

福州路上的公司大减价广告

The advertisement for sales on Fuzhou Road

● 1998 年建于福州路的上海书城

● Shanghai bookstore built on Fuzhou Road in 1998

八 其他街区 Other Blocks

● 都城饭店 1935 年建成开业，1964 年更名为新城饭店

● Metropole Hotel was opened in 1935 and changed its name to Xincheng Hotel in 1964

● 重建于 1914 年的工部局大楼，此处为福州路江西路口

● The building of Municipal Council was reconstructed in 1914 and now this site is the intersection of Fuzhou Road and Jiangxi Road

工部局大楼，1949年10月2日上海市人民政府在此升起全市第一面五星红旗

This is the building of Municipal Council where the first Five-star Red Flag was raised by the Shanghai Municipal People's Government on Oct.2,1949

位于九江路江西路口的加利饭店和电话大楼

Kallee Hotel and the Telephone Building on the intersection of Jiujiang Road and Jiangxi Road

八

其他街区 Other Blocks

● 圣三一堂始建于1847年，1866年在汉口路江西路重建

● Holy Trinity Church was established in 1847 and reconstructed on Hankou Road and Jiangxi Road in 1866

● 广东路街景

● The street scene on Guangdong Road

● 广西路上的凤桂茶园

● Fenggui Tea House on Guangxi Road

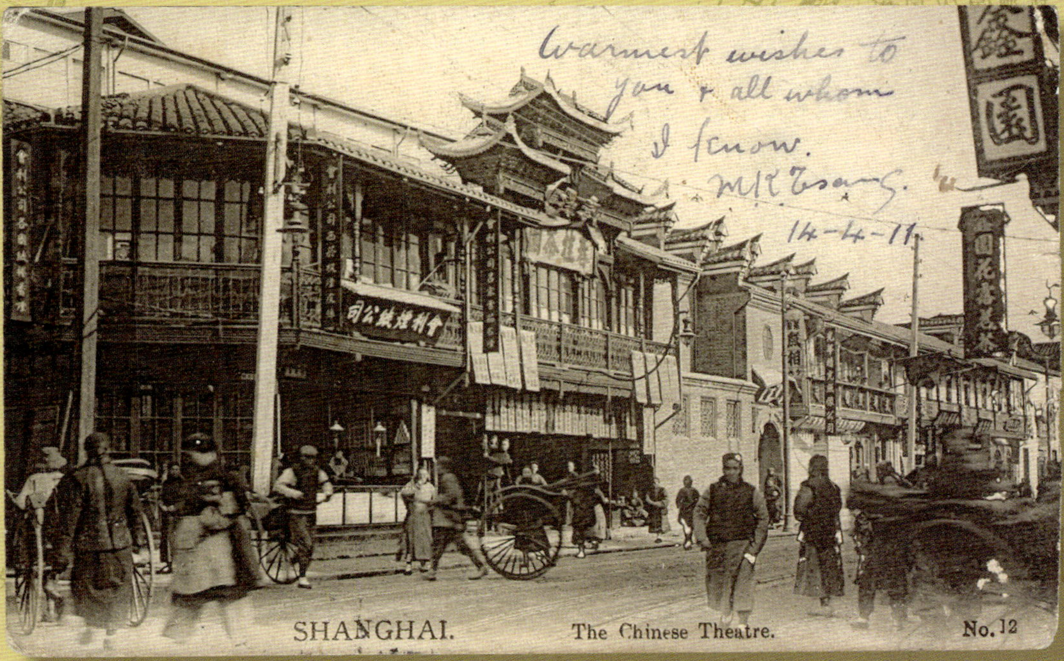

● 汉口路湖北路口的春桂茶园

● Chungui Tea House on the intersection of Hankou Road and Hubei Road

八

其他街区 Other Blocks

西藏路原是沿泥城浜的一条土路

Xizang Road was once an earth road along Nichengbang

1914 年填浜筑路后，西藏路成为租界内南北向主干道

The creek was filled in 1914 and Xizang Road became a north—south main road in the concession

- 1936 年西藏路改名为虞洽卿路，1943 年又复名西藏路
- Xizang Road was renamed as Yu Qiaqing Road in 1936 and resumed Xizang Road in 1943

八

其他街区 Other Blocks

● 1929 年建于西藏路的东方饭店，1950 年改为上海工人文化宫

● The Oriental Hotel built on Xizang Road in 1929 was changed to Shanghai Worker's Cultural Palace in 1950

● 20世纪60年代的上海工人文化宫

● Shanghai Worker's Cultural Palace in the 1960s

20世纪80年代的上海工人文化宫

Shanghai Worker's Cultural Palace in the 1980s

1968年在西藏路开业的星火日夜商店，是上海第一家24小时营业的商店

Xinghuo day-and-night shop opened on Xizang Road in 1968 is Shanghai's first shop that opens 24 hours a day

1931 年建于西藏路的慕尔堂，1958 年改称沐恩堂

Mu Er Tang built on Xizang Road in 1931 was renamed as Mu En Tang in 1958

沐恩堂全景

A full view of Mu En Tang

20世纪80年代的西藏路远景

The full view of Xizang Road in the 1980s

21世纪初的西藏路远景

The full view of Xizang Road in the 2000s

洋泾浜原为黄浦江支流，是英法租界的界河

Yangjingbang, once a ramification of Huangpu River, was the boundary river of the British Concession and French Concession

清末的洋泾浜

Yangjingbang in the late Qing Dynasty

洋泾浜沿岸由早期的棚户区逐步建成商行、旅店

The early shanty town was changed to shops and hotels along Yangjingbang

洋泾浜沿岸的旅店

Hotels along Yangjingbang

八

其他街区 Other Blocks

大清朱家角邮局

● 洋泾浜大安栈的近景

● The close shot of Da An Hotel along Yangjingbang

● 洋泾浜大安栈的远景

● The distant view of Da An Hotel along Yangjingbang

- 洋泾浜成为中西商贸的前沿之地，中西文化的交流，衍生出"洋泾浜英语"
- Yangjingbang became the advancing front for Chinese and western businesses and the communication between China and western countriesd generate Pidgin English

- 洋泾浜两岸的中西建筑
- Chinese and western-style architectures on both sides of Yangjingbang

八

其他街区

Other Blocks

大清朱家角邮局

1915 年洋泾浜被填浜筑路，命名为爱多亚路

In 1915 Yangjingbang was filled to pave road and the road was called Avenue Edward VII

填浜后的爱多亚路

Avenue Edward VII

● 外滩爱多亚路口，1950 年爱多亚路改名为延安东路

● The Bund at the intersection of Avenue Edward VII Avenue. The Avonue was renamed as East Yan'an Road in 1950

● 1997 年建成通向外滩的延安路高架下匝道

● Off-Ramp of Yan'an Road Viaduct leading to the Bund was built in 1997

八 其他街区 Other Blocks

建于1917年的大世界游艺场，位于爱多亚路西藏路口

The Great World Entertainment Centre built in 1917 on the intersection of Avenue Edward VII and Xizang Road

大世界游艺场旧景

An old scene of the Great World Entertainment Centre

- 大世界游艺场内景
- The indoor scene of The Great World Entertainment Centre

- 1924年重建的大世界游艺场
- The Great World Entertainment Centre was reconstructed in 1924

1954 年大世界游艺场改名为人民游乐场

The Great World Entertainment Centre was renamed as people's pleasure ground in 1954

1960 年人民游乐场的夜景

The night scene of the people's pleasure ground in 1960

● 1974 年人民游乐场改名为青年宫

● People's pleasure ground was renamed as youth palace in 1974

● 1987 年青年宫改名为大世界游乐中心

● Youth palace was renamed as Great World Entertainment Centre in 1987

建于1930年的南京大戏院，1959年改名为上海音乐厅

Nanjing Grand Theater built in 1930 was renamed as Shanghai Concert Hall in 1959

2003年上海音乐厅向南整体平移60多米

Shanghai Concert Hall was repositioned for a distance of more than 60 meters southward in 2003

● 建于1909年的爱俪园，又称哈同花园，20世纪30年代损毁

● Aili Garden built in 1909, also called Hardoon's Garden was damagd in the 1930s

● 1955年在哈同花园原址建上海中苏友好大厦，1968 年改名为上海展览馆

● Shanghai Sino—Soviet friendship building was built on this site in 1955 and it was renamed as Shanghai Exhibition Hall in 1968

● 1984年上海展览馆改名为上海展览中心，是上海举行大型活动的重要场所

● Shanghai Exhibition Hall was renamed as Shanghai Exhibition Center in 1984 as an important venue for large—scale activities

20 世纪 50 年代的中苏友好大厦工业馆

Industrial Exhibition Hall of Sino-Soviet Friendship Building in the 1950s

20 世纪 70 年代在上海展览馆举办的工业展览会

Polytechnic exhibition held in the hall in the 1970s

马勒住宅始建于1915年，是一座模仿邮船样式的建筑

Moller House was built in 1915 which was a post boat style building

嘉道理住宅始建于1919年，又称大理石大厦，1953年划归中国福利会作为少年宫

Kadoorie House also called the" Grand Marble House" was built in 1919. It was incorporated in China Welfare Institute as children's palace in 1953

● 建于1987年的静安希尔顿大酒店是上海第一家五星级的宾馆

● Hilton Hotel in Jing'An district built in 1987 was the first 5-star hotel in Shanghai

● 上海国际贵都大饭店1991年建成

● Hotel Equatorial Shanghai was built in 1991

20世纪60年代的延安中路

Middle Yan'an Road in the 1960s

20世纪90年代的延安中路

Middle Yan'an Road in the 1990s

● 1999年建成的延安中路高架

● Middle Yan'an Road overhead viaduct was built in 1999

● 1999年14.8公里长的延安高架路全线建成通车

● The whole line of Yan'an elevated road about 14.8 kilometers was opened to traffic in 1999.

徐家汇因肇嘉浜、蒲汇塘和法华泾三水汇合而得名

Xujiahui gained the name because Zhaojiabang, Puhuitang and Fahuajing converged there

徐光启纪念馆 2005 年重新开馆

Xu Guangqi commemorative museum was reopened in 2005

早期徐家汇的河湾与小桥

The embayment and bridge in Xujiahui

建于1872年的徐家汇天文台

Xujiahui observatory built in 1872

八

其他街区 Other Blocks

● 徐家汇土山湾孤儿工艺院，1906 年为比利时承建的中国宫

● Tushanwan Orphan Artifact Institution in Xujiahui was the Chinese Pavilion built for Belgium in 1906

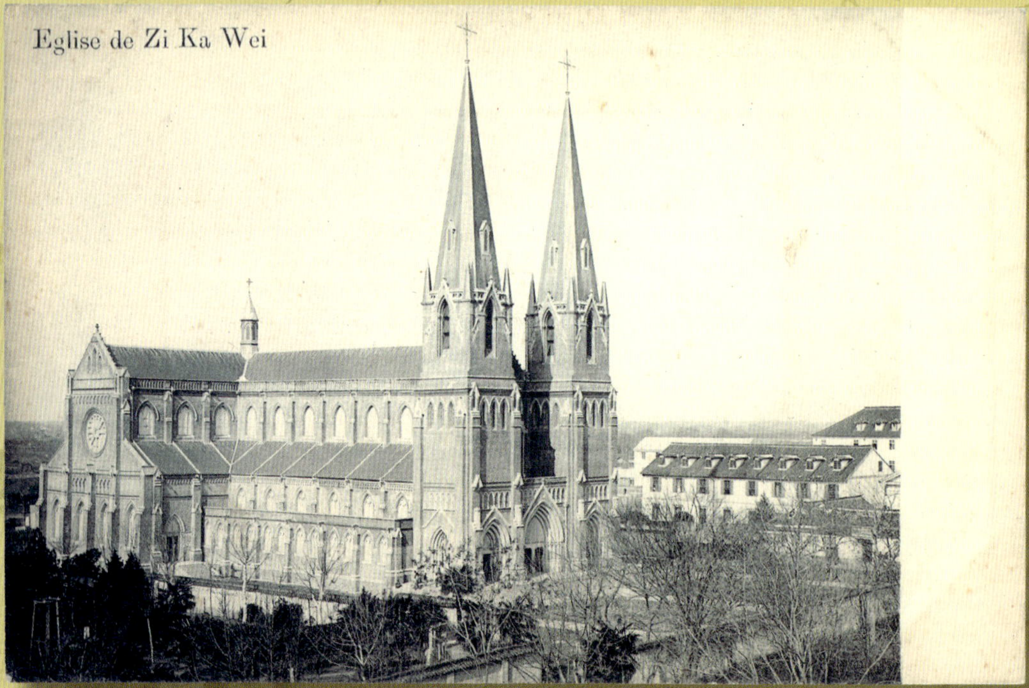

● 1906 年新建的徐家汇天主教堂

● The newly built Xujiahua Christianity church in 1906

21世纪初的徐家汇天主教堂的内外景

The indoor and outdoor scene of Xujiahui Christianity church in the 2000s

创办于1850年的徐汇中学新貌

A new look of Xuhui middle school founded in 1850

1847年建于徐家汇的藏书楼，是上海现存最早的图书馆

The library built in Xujiahui in 1847 was the earliest extant library in Shanghai

SICCAWEI-CREEK OF SHANGHAI.

● 水渐干涸并严重污染的肇嘉浜

● The water of Zhaojiabang dried up gradually and was severely polluted.

● 1956 年填浜筑路建成肇嘉浜交通干道

● It was filled to pave road in 1956 forming a main road of Zhaojiabang

八 其他街区 Other Blocks

● 20世纪60年代的徐家汇

● Xujiahui in the 1960s

● 20世纪90年代的徐家汇

● Xujiahui in the 1990s

2000年的徐家汇商业中心

Xujiahui Commercial center in 2000

21世纪初的徐家汇夜景

The night scene of Xujiahui in the 2000s

八 其他街区 Other Blocks

● 建于1975年可容纳1.8万人的上海体育馆

● Shanghai Indoor Stadium built in 1975 can hold 18,000 people

● 建于1997年可容纳8万人的上海体育场

● Shanghai Stadium built in 1997 can hold 80,000 people

徐汇花园住宅远眺

A distant view of Garden-like Residence in Xuhui

徐家汇公园远眺

A distant view of XuJiahui Park

20 世纪初的龙华塔

Longhua Tower in the 1900s

20 世纪 30 年代的龙华塔

Longhua Tower in the 1930s

龙华寺大殿旧貌

The old scene of Longhua Temple

千年古刹龙华寺，历经战火多次重建

The ancient Buddhist temple Longhua Temple was reconstructed for many times with the baptism of warfares

龙华寺内的佛像

Figure of Buddha in Longhua Temple

龙华寺内景

The indoor scene of Longhua Temple

20世纪30年代的龙华寺

Longhua Temple in the 1930s

20世纪90年代的龙华寺

Longhua Temple in the 1990s

● 1995年重建于龙华的烈士陵园

● Longhua Cemetery of Revolutionary Martyrs reconstructed in 1995

- 21 世纪初的龙华胜景
- The wonderful scenery of Longhua in the 2000s

八

其他街区 Other Blocks

● 龙华寺春、冬景色

● The scene of spring and winter in Longhua Temple

Village Scene. Kiangwan.

- 江湾因吴淞江蜿蜒流过而得名
- Jiangwan gained the name because Wusong River passed there

Village Scene. Kiangwan.

清末江湾老镇

The old town in Jiangwan in the late Qing Dynasty

1911 年由华人自办的江湾跑马厅，后改名为万国体育馆

Jiangwan racecourse run by Chinese in 1911 was renamed the International Indoor Stadium afterwards

● 1937 年侵略上海的日军在江湾的炮阵地

● The Japanese Army who invaded Shanghai in 1937 at the artillery position of Jiangwan

● 1937 年江湾跑马厅毁于战火

● Jiangwan racecourse was destroyed in war in 1937

1926 年新开辟的江湾五角场

Jiangwan Intersection Circle newly opened in 1926

2006 年的江湾五角场中心广场夜景

The night scene of the center square of Wu Jiao Chang in 2006

- 20世纪30年代在江湾新建设的市中心区
- The newly built Jaingwan downtown in the 1930s

- 1933年上海市政府新厦建成
- The new building of Shanghai municipal government in 1933

1937年市政府新厦在战火中受损，今为上海体育学院办公楼

The new building of Shanghai municipal government was destroyed in warfare, Now it is the office building of Shanghai University of Sport

上海特别市政府1927年在平江路成立，1937年后搬回原址办公

The Government of Shanghai Special City was established on Pingjiang Road in 1927 and after 1937 it was moved to the former site

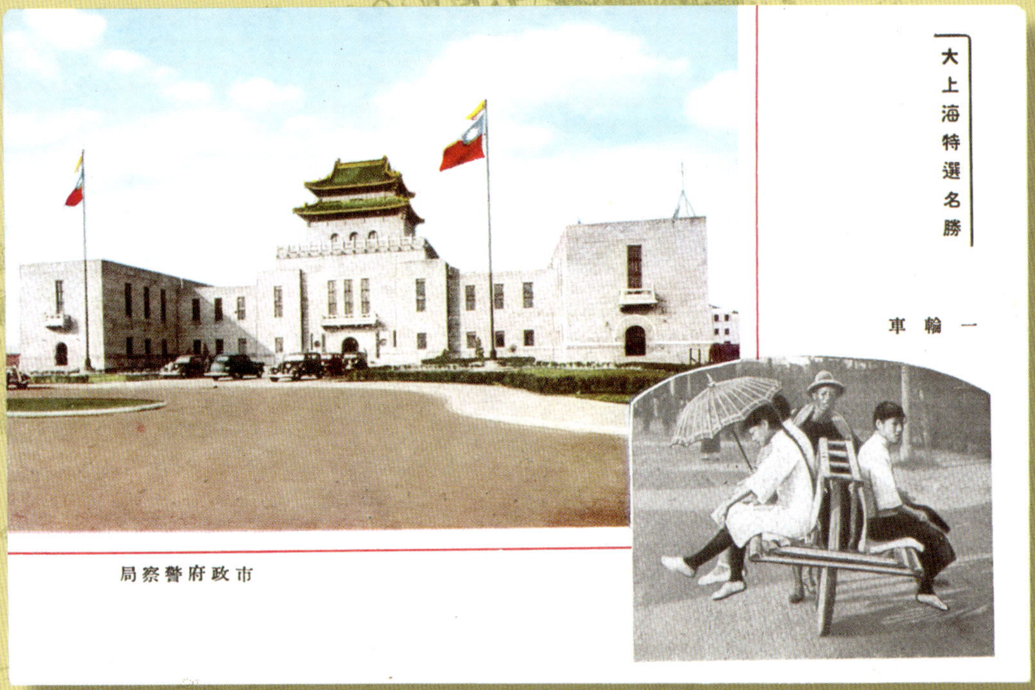

● 1936年建成的上海市图书馆，曾作为市警察局

● Shanghai Library built in 1936 was once the police department of Shanghai

● 1937年改作上海民国维新政府，今为同济中学图书馆

● It was renamed as Shanghai Reformed Government of the Republic of China in 1937 and now it is the library of Tongji Middle School

1936 年建成的上海市博物馆

Shanghai Museum built in 1936

上海市博物馆今为长海医院影像楼

Now Shanghai Museum is the Image Building of Changhai Hospital

1935 年建成的上海市运动场

Shanghai playground built in 1935

1935 年上海市运动场举办了第六届全国运动会

The sixth national games was held in Shanghai playground in 1935

上海市體育館　Gymnasium of Greater Shanghai.

● 建于1935年的上海市体育馆

● Shanghai Indoor Stadium built in 1935

上海市游泳池大門　Entrance to the Swimming Pool of Greater Shanghai.

● 建于1935年的上海市游泳池

● Shanghai Swimming Pool built in 1935

1935 年上海市运动场大门

Portal of Shanghai playground in 1935

1956 年上海市运动场改名为上海市江湾体育场

Shanghai playground was renamed as Shanghai Jiangwan Stadium in 1956

1936 年建航空协会会所，俗称飞机楼

The club of Airline Association was built in 1936 which was commonly called airplane building

复旦大学1905 年创办，1922 年迁至江湾新校址

Fudan University was established in 1905 and moved to the new site in Jiangwan in 1922

1937 年复旦大学被日军占领

Fudan University was occupied by Japanese Army in 1937

复旦大学图书馆遭战火破坏

The library of Fudan University was destroyed in warfare

2005 年复旦大学建校一百周年纪念

100th anniversary of the foundaing of Fudan University in 2005

2007 年同济大学建校一百周年纪念

100th anniversary of the foundaing of Tongji University in 2007

清末的杨树浦路

Yangshupu Road in the late Qing Dynasty

杨树浦路上的有轨电车

The streetcar on Yangshupu Road

大清朱家角邮局

杨树浦的河与桥

The rivers and bridges of Yangshupu

杨树浦的河与桥

The rivers and bridges of Yangshupu

20 世纪 10 年代的杨树浦路街景

The street scene of Yangshupu Road in the 1910s

1932 年日军侵占杨树浦

Japanese army invaded Yangshupu in 1932

建于1883年的上海自来水公司水厂

The water plant of Shanghai Waterworks Company built in 1883

上海自来水公司水厂内景

The indoor scene of Shanghai Waterworks Company

建于 1913 年的杨树浦发电厂

Yangshupu power plant built in 1913

21 世纪初的杨树浦水厂新貌

The new look of Yangshupu water plant in the 2000s

八

其他街区 Other Blocks

1891 年华人在铁马路建钱业会馆。1925 年增建钱业公学，解放后改为新中中学

Qianye hall was built by Chinese on Tiema Road in 1891. Qianye public school was built in 1925 which was renamed as Xinzhong Middle School after liberation

1998 年迁建于原平路的新中高级中学

Xinzhong Senior Middle School was moved and built on Yuanping Road in 1998

1932 年大场镇上的断壁残垣

The dilapidated walls of Dachang Town in 1932

1924 年建于宝山路的东方图书馆，1932 年遭日军炮击而毁

The Oriental Library built on Baoshan Road in 1924 was destroyed by the bombardment of Japanese army in 1932

八

其他街区 Other Blocks

大清朱家角邮局

1937年广中路成为激战之地

Guangzhong Road became a place with fierce battles in 1937

1937年宝山路上的商务印书馆毁于战火

Commercial Press on Baoshan Road was destroyed in war in 1937

- 1937年宝山路成为激战之地
- Baoshan Road became a site of fierce battles in 1937

- 激战后的宝山路
- Baoshan Road after fierce battles

八 其他街区 Other Blocks

清末新闸路街景

The street scene of Xinzha Road in the late Qing Dynasty

清末卡德路街景，今石门二路

Street scene of Carter Road in the late Qing Dynasty (The current No.2 Shi Men Road)

● 极司菲而路，今万航渡路

● Jessfield Road, the current Wanhangdu Road

● 位于极司菲而路上的同仁医院

● Tongren Hospital located on Jessfield Road

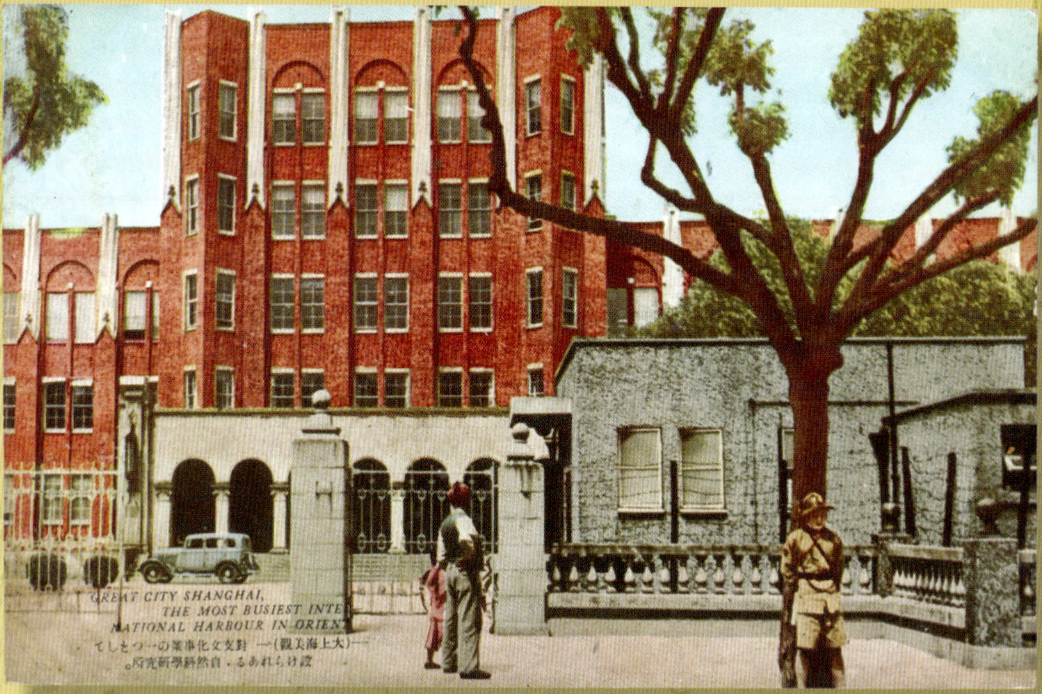

建于1931年的上海自然科学研究所

Shanghai Research Institute of Natural Sciences built in 1931

1958年在岳阳路成立的中国科学院上海分院

Chinese Academy of Science Shanghai Branch built on Yueyang Road in 1958

建于1937年的普希金纪念碑，位于今岳阳路、汾阳路、桃江路、东平路的交界处

Pushkin commemorative plaque built in 1937 was located on the center of the juncture of the current Yueyang Road, Fenyang Road, Taojiang Road, and Dongping Road

普希金纪念碑曾两次被毁，1987年在原址重建

The commemorative plaque was destroyed twice and reconstructed on the former site in 1987

八

其他街区 Other Blocks

大清朱家角邮局

● 上海中学的前身为始建于1865年的龙门书院

● The predecessor of Shanghai High School was Long Men College built in 1865

● 建于1956年的上海市跳伞塔，位于控江路打虎山路口，1989年拆除

● Shanghai parachute tower built in 1956 was located on the intersection of Kongjiang Road and Dahushan Road which was knocked down in 1989

● 河南南路上的中汇大楼曾为上海博物馆
● Zhonghui Building on South Henan Road was once Shanghai Museum

● 汾阳路上的上海工艺美术博物馆
● Shanghai Arts & Crafts Museum on Fenyang Road

20世纪30年代的虹桥路

Hongqiao Road in the 1930s

始建于1983年的虹桥开发区是中国最早的经济技术开发区

Hongqiao Development Area established in 1983 was China's earliest Economic and Technical Development Area

建于1999年的上海马戏城

Shanghai Circus World built in 1999

上海站不夜城

Shanghai Station, sleepless night town

八

其他街区

Other Blocks

大清朱家角郵局

● 云南路美食街

● Yunan Road Food Street

● 黄河路美食街

● Huanghe Road Food Street

POST CARD

POST

衡山路街景

The street scene of Hengshan Road

衡山路休闲街

Hengshan Road Food Street

八 其他街区 Other Blocks

雁荡路休闲街

Leisure Street on Yandang Road

吴江路休闲街

Food Street on Wujiang Road

● 上海影城 1991 年建于番禺路，1993 年在此举办首届上海国际电影节

● Shanghai Film Art Center was built on Fanyu Road in 1991 where the first Shanghai International Film Festival was held in 1993

● 愚园路历史文化风貌区

● Yuyuan Road historical and cultural area

八

其他街区

Other Blocks

思南路秋景

The autumn scene on Sinan Road

思南路雪景

The snowscape on Sinan Road

九

交通发展

Transportation Development

上海的水系发达，航运条件优越，居民以舟代步、枕河而居。上海在开埠前已是中国最大的航运交通枢纽和沿海贸易港口。随着陆路交通的发展，传统和现代交通工具的共处、更替及道路的拓展，上海成为交通工具的实验场。同时，车轮的转动给城市注入了活力，也改变着人们的生活节奏。上海的交通发展与城市的兴盛相辅相成，互为促进。如今，地上和地下、水面和空中、专线和环线、聚集和辐射，构成了现代化的城市立体交通网。上海的魅力在于流动，交通的发展使上海生机盎然。

Shanghai owns a well-developed water system and predominant shipping condition where the dwellers use boats as a means of transportation and live by the river. Shanghai was already the largest maritime hub, transport hub and coasting trade port in China before it opened the port. With the development of land communications, the coexistence, alteration of traditional and modern vehicles and the extension of road, Shanghai has become a test site for transportation. Meanwhile, the motion of the wheels injects vitality into the city and changes people's life rhythm. The transportation development and the flourishing of the city are complementary to each other. Nowadays, below and ground traffic system, surface and air traffic system, special and loop line, aggregation and radiation form a modern multilevel traffic net of the city. The charm of Shanghai rests with movement and the development of transportation makes Shanghai full of vigor.

以船为居，以船为业

Living and working by boats

一根竹篙撑起一个家

One bamboo spar can support one family

● 沙船是上海航运的先驱

● Junk was the forerunner of the shipping business in Shanghai

● 沙船集结帆樯如林

● Concentration of junks and a forest of masts

九

交通发展 Transportation Development

十六铺的帆船

Sailbats on Shiliupu

十六铺为上海港的发源地

Shiliupu was the cradle land of the Port of Shanghai

● 码头边的摊贩

● Hawkers by the wharf

● 劳动中的码头工人

● Dockers were working

码头上装卸货物的情景

The scene of handling goods on the wharf

码头上的西瓜市场

Watermelon market on the wharf

十六铺集市

Market in Shiliupu

十六铺集市

Market in Shiliupu

九

交通发展 Transportation Development

大清朱家角邮局

● 码头上的茶铺与粥摊

● Tea shop and Rice Gruel Stand on the wharf

● 外滩沿江的渡船码头

● The ferry berth on the bund along the river

● 外滩沿江的渡船码头

● The ferry berth on the bund along the river

大清朱家角郵局

● 英租界外滩栈桥

● The landing piers of the British Bund

● 法租界外滩栈桥

● The landing piers of the French Bund

码头边停泊的舢舨

The sampan by the wharf

驳船码头

Barge berth

始建于1845年的汇山码头，早年鲁迅、郭沫若从这里登船东渡日本求学

Huishan Wharf was built in 1845. Lu Xun and Guo Moruo left for Japan from here for further study in their early years

1937年黄浦、杨树浦、华顺码头统称为汇山码头

Huangpu Wharf, Yangshupu Wharf, Huashun Wharf were collectively called Huishan Wharf in 1937

● 上海石油化工总厂陈山原油码头

● Chenshan crude oil wharf of Shanghai Petroleum Chemical Engineering Corporation

● 1995 年芦潮港码头建成

● The wharf of Luchao Port was accomplished in 1995

九

交通发展 Transportation Development

苏州河上的货运船

Freight vessels on Suzhou River

苏州河上的货运船

Freight vessels on Suzhou River

黄浦江上的货运船

Freight vessels on Huangpu River

黄浦江上的货运船

Freight vessels on Huangpu River

九

交通发展 Transportation Development

黄浦江上的摆渡船

Ferries on Huangpu River

黄浦江上的客运船

Passenger-transporting boats on Huangpu River

便当的民渡舢舨

Convenient sampan for transporting passengers

黄浦江上的民渡舢舨

Convenient sampan on Huangpu River

九

交通发展 Transportation Development

1910年开办市轮渡

The ferry business of the city was established in 1910

20世纪80年代的浦江轮渡

The ferryboat on Huangpu River in the 1980s

浦江上的游览船

Sightseeing boats on Huangpu River

浦江上的游览船

Sightseeing boats on Huangpu River

● 乡间的泥土路
● Muddy roads in the country

● 泥土路上的行人
● Muddy roads and Pedestrians in the country

乘坐马车外出踏青的侨民

The immigrants were going for an outing in the country in spring

乘坐木船外出游玩的侨民

The immigrants on an outing by wooden boats

早期的泥土街道

A clay street in early days

以石板铺设的道路

Street paved by flagstone

弹硌路是用石子铺设的路

Cobblestone road is paved by stones

1907 年南京路曾使用铁藜木砖铺设路面

Nanjing Road was paved by bricks made of common mesua in 1907

九 交通发展 Transportation Development

大清朱家角郵局

● 用煤渣铺成的路面

● Road surface paved by cinder

● 铺设柏油马路

● Asphalt roads were being paved

● 1917年福建路建成上海第一条水泥马路

● The first concrete road in Shanghai was built in 1917 on Fujian Road

● 用砖铺设的路面

● The brick-paved road

牧童来去黄牛背

The buffalo boy on the back of the water buffalo

骑在牛背上的牧牛人

The cowherd on the back of the water buffalo

- 街市上骑马的巡警
- The policemen on horsebacks in the street

- 骑马的印度巡捕
- The Indian patrolmen on horsebacks

九

交通发展 Transportation Development

大清朱家角邮局

轿子是早期的代步工具

Sedan chair was the vehicle in an early period

轿子是早期的代步工具

Sedan chair was the vehicle in an early period

1855 年马车出现在上海滩

The carriage appeared in Shanghai in 1855

络绎不绝的马车

The busy traffic of carriages

九

交通发展 Transportation Development

1862年以后独轮车兴盛一时

Wheelbarrow was prevalent for a time after 1862

坐独轮车出行的妇女儿童

Women and children on wheel barrow

一帆风顺的独轮车

Wheelbarrows ran before the wind

外滩当年的“出租车队”

The taxi fleet on the Bund that year

九 交通发展 Transportation Development

1874 年上海引进人力车

The man-drawn vehicle was introduced in Shanghai in 1874

1913 年人力车改称黄包车

It was renamed as rickshaw in 1913

城内待客的黄包车

Rickshaws in the city waiting for the passengers

路边待客的黄包车

Rickshaws waiting by the road

九

交通发展 Transportation Development

大清朱家角郵局

1869 年自行车进入上海

Bike was introduced into Shanghai in 1869

Street Scene in Shanghai Northwest Orient Airlines

1923 年三轮车开始发展起来

Tricycle was developed in 1923

自行车曾是大众化的交通工具

Bike was once the popular vehicle

光新路口浩浩荡荡的自行车队伍

The army of bicycle riders on Guangxin Road

● 建于1876年的吴淞铁路，是中国第一条营运铁路

● Wusong Railway built in 1876 was the first railway in service in China

● 1876年7月3日吴淞铁路通车时的场景

● Wusong Railway's open to traffic on July 3rd, 1876

观看火车的人们

People watching trains

21 世纪初驶于上海站的东风内燃机车

Dongfeng railway motor car was running from Shanghai Station in the 2000s

1897 年重建淞沪铁路，此为当年上海站，位于今天目东路

Songhu Railway was reconstructed in 1897 and this was Shanghai Railway Station that time

1908 年沪宁铁路通车，此为上海北火车站

Shanghai– Nanjing Railway was opened to traffic in 1908. This was the north station of Shanghai Railway Station

● 民国时期的北火车站

● North railway station in the period of the Republic of China

● 1932 年、1937 年北火车站两度遭日军轰炸

● Shanghai North Railway Station was bombed twice by the Japanese Army in 1932 and 1937

九 交通发展 Transportation Development

● 北站和铁道管理局在战火中受损

● North railway station and railway administrative bureau were damaged during the battle

● 20 世纪 50 年代的北火车站，1987 年北火车站停止使用

● North railway station in the 1950s， Shanghai North Railway Station went out of service in 1987

● 2004 年仿老北站建成的上海铁路博物馆

● Shanghai Railway Museum was established in 2004 copying the style of the old Shanghai North Railway Station

九

交通发展
Transportation Development

1987 年在东站原址建上海新火车站

The new Shanghai Railway Station was built on the former site of the east station in 1987

20 世纪 90 年代的上海火车站

Shanghai Railway Station in the 1990s

21 世纪初的上海站新貌

The new look of Shanghai Railway Station in the 2000s

位于不夜城地区的上海火车站远眺

A distant view of Shanghai Railway Station located on the sleepless city of Shanghai

九
交通发展
Transportation Development

建于1908年的上海南火车站，原址位于南车站路

Shanghai South Railway Station was built in 1908 and the former site was on South Station Road

1909年沪杭甬铁路通车

Shanghai–Hangzhou–Ningbo Railway was opened to traffic in 1909

1937 年上海南站被日军炸毁

Shanghai South Railway Station was bombed out by the Japanese Army in 1937

2006 年建成的新上海南站

The new Shanghai South Railway Station was built in 2006

1901 年汽车第一次进入上海

Automobile entered Shanghai for the first time in 1901

1930 年汽车在积水的浙江路上行驶

The car was running on the waterish Zhejiang Road in 1930

- 1908年有轨电车正式运营
- The streetcar was put into service in 1908

- 首条电车线路由静安寺经南京路至广东路外滩
- The first street car line ran from Jing'an Temple to the Bund at Guangdong Road passing Nanjing Road

九

交通发展 Transportation Development

1914年第一条无轨电车线路通车

The first railless tram car was opened in 1914

行驶在西藏路上的18路无轨电车

No.18 trolleybus was running on Xizang Road

● 1922 年公共汽车开通，1 路车由今中山公园至虹口公园

● Bus was opened into operation in 1922. No.1 bus runs from Zhongshan Park to Hongkou Park

● 1934 年双层公共汽车开通

● The two deck bus was put into service in 1934

双层公共汽车在南京路上行驶

The two story bus was running on Nanjing Road

南京路上的各种车辆

All kinds of vehicles on Nanjing Road

行驶在南京路上的电车

Street cars were running on Nanjing Road

行驶在吴淞路上的卡车

The truck was running on Wusong Road

九

交通发展

Transportation Development

● 用于巡逻的摩托车

● Patrol motorcycles

● 用于巡逻的警车

● Patrol cars

- 19 世纪 80 年代创制的运货塌车
- Manpower freight vehicle made in the 1880s

- 运货塌车
- Freight vehicle

沪太路上的大场汽车站

Dachang Bus Station on Hutai Road

1956年建于共和新路上的上海第一座车行立交桥

The first overpass for vehicle in Shanghai built on Gonghexin Road in 1956

20 世纪 60 年代的张庙路

Zhangmiao Road in the 1960s

20 世纪 60 年代的闵行 1 号路

No.1 Road in Minhang in the 1960s

建于1922年的龙华机场

Longhua Airport built in 1922

1929年上海开启民航运输

Shanghai opened civil aviation transport in 1929

- 20 世纪 40 年代，飞越城市上空的飞机
- The airplane was flying over the city in the 1940s

- 1937 年 8 月 13 号日军借口虹桥机场事件，在上海发动战争
- Japanese army waged war in Shanghai on the excuse of the Hongqiao Airport incident on August 13th, 1937

1963 年虹桥机场重建为民用机场

Hongqiao Airport was rebuilt into a civil airport in 1963

虹桥机场停机坪

The parking ground of Hongqiao Airport

● 始建于1997年的浦东国际机场

● Pudong International Airport built in 1997

● 上海建有虹桥、浦东两个国际机场

● There are two international airports in Shanghai — Hongqiao Airport and Pudong International Airport

1995年上海第一条地铁交通线开通

The first subway line in Shanghai was opened in 1995

地铁人民广场站

MTR station at People's Square

- 地铁 2 号线科技馆站外景
- The outer door scene of Shanghai Technology Museum Station of Line 2

- 2010 年上海建成有 10 条轨道交通线，在建有 3 条
- Shanghai has built 10 subway lines and 3 more under way till 2010

建于 2000 年的外滩观光隧道

Sightseeing Tunnel at the Bund built in 2000

建于 2000 年的轻轨交通线

The traffic line of the light rail built in 2000

● 2003年世界第一条商业运营的磁悬浮列车线开通

● The first commercial operative line of Maglev train in the world was opened in 2003

九

交通发展 Transportation Development

1991 年建成的吴淞路闸桥于 2009 年拆除

The Gate Bridge on Wusong Road built in 1991 was removed in 2009

1990 年上海内环高架路开始施工，内环线全长 45 公里，1994 年建成通车

The construction of Shanghai Inner Ring Viaduct started in 1990 with a length of 45 kilometers and it was opened to traffic in 1994

上海体育馆附近的内环高架路

Inner Ring Viaduct near Shanghai Gymnasium

九

交通发展 Transportation Development

沪青平高速公路

Huqingping Highway

虹桥开发区道路

The Road of Hongqiao Development Zone

● 延安高架与南北高架路
● Yan'an Road Viaduct and the North–South Viaduct

● 内环高架与南北高架路
● The Inner Ring Viaduct road and the North–South Viaduct

九

交通发展 Transportation Development

延安高架路的夜景

The night scene of Yan'an Road Viaduct

延安高架路的夜景

The night scene of Yan'an Road Viaduct

浦东的高架路

Viaduct in Pudong District

浦东的高架路

Viaduct in Pudong District

浦东世纪大道

The Century Avenue in Pudong District

浦东世纪大道夜景

The night scene of Century Avenue

通往洋山港的东海大桥建于2005年，全长32.5公里

Donghai Bridge leading to Yangshan Port was built in 2005 with a total length of 32.5 kilometers

洋山深水港于2005年建成使用

Yangshan deep-water port was established and put into service in 2005

通往崇明的长江遂桥建于2009年，全长25.5公里

Yangtze River Tunnel leading to Chongming Island was built in 2009 with a total length of 25.5 kilometers

夕阳下的东海大桥

Donghai Bridge in the sunset

十

城乡风貌

Urban and Rural Scenery

8m 11 *Peach Blossoms and the Pagoda at Long Hou Shangai.* 上海の景

何为城，何为乡？对于上海这个百年巨变的城市来说，确实难以划定。原来的上海县城以相围的城墙和护城河为边界，现在的上海大部分城区当时还是郊野，浦东更是一派田园景象。城乡的边缘线在逐步扩展，城市的天际线在渐渐升高，上海城市形态的变化和辉煌的历史，连接着这座城市的过去与现在，并预示着美好的未来。科教兴市、浦东开发、世博盛会为上海文明、生态、智慧城市建设带来机遇。上海这个海纳百川、兼容并蓄的国际大都市，将以崭新的风貌屹立在东方之滨。

What is a city? What is a village? It is really difficult to delimit for Shanghai because it has undergone great changes during the last several hundred years. The Boundary of former Shanghai County was the surrounded city walls and the moat. Most part of Shanghai today was suburbs at that time and Pudong was an area of fields and gardens. The edge line between the city and the village was extended gradually and the skyline of the city was heightened. The development of the configuration in Shanghai and the brilliant history connected the past and present of this city indicating a rosy future. The city's revitalization through science and education, the development of Pudong and the World Expo pageant bring opportunities for this civilized, ecological and sapiential city. Shanghai, the cosmopolitan city will stand on the bank of the East with a new look.

十

城乡风貌 Urban and Rural Scenery

● 清末上海乡镇

● Villages and towns of Shanghai in the late Qing Dynasty

清末上海乡村

The village of Shanghai in the late Qing Dynasty

清末上海乡村

The village of Shanghai in the late Qing Dynasty

乡村清澈的河水

Limpid river water in the village

乡村的道路

The country road

乡村的桥

The bridge of the county

乡村的桥

The bridge of the county

十

城乡风貌

Urban and Rural Scenery

大清朱家角邮局

205. - Environs de Shanghai. - Une Crique — *Shanghai Suburbs. - A creek*

Cliché R. Tillot

CREEK SCENE AROUND SHANGHAI 上海郊外のクリーク

● 上海郊外风景

● The suburban landscape of Shanghai

上海郊外风景

The suburban landscape of Shanghai

上海郊外风景

The suburban landscape of Shanghai

上海的牌楼

The decorated archway of Shanghai

上海的牌坊

The memorial arches of Shanghai

● 清末大户人家的宅门

● Gate of the rich family in the late Qing Dynasty

● 屋顶上的塔型装饰建筑

● Tower-shaped decorative architecture on the roof

庙宇

Temples

牌楼

Decorated archway

- 庙宇和牌楼
- Temples and decorated archway

大清朱家角邮局

- 1900 年始建玉佛寺，寺内坐佛像
- Jade Buddha Temple of was built in 1900. The figure of the sitting Buddha in the temple

- 1928 年重建玉佛寺
- Jade Buddha Temple of was rebuilt in 1928

玉佛寺内的大雄宝殿

The main palace in the Jade Buddha Temple

玉佛寺内的卧佛像

Figure of reclined Buddha in the Jade Buddha Temple

● 庙宇里供奉的佛像

● Figures of Buddha enshrined in the temple

● 当年被人们崇拜的神像

● Figures of Buddha worshipped by people at that time

河边捕鱼

Fishing by the river side

河边饲养

Feeding by the river side

乡村的水田

Paddy field in the country

乡村的水田

Paddy field in the country

十 城乡风貌 Urban and Rural Scenery

大清朱家角郵局

引水灌田

Irrigating the fields

耕作的村民

Villagers were working

● 踩水车灌田

● Manpowered Waterwheel was irrigating the fields

● 打谷的村民

● Villagers were threshing

吴淞乡下房屋

Rural houses in Wusong

宝山县学堂

School in Baoshan County

● 1932年宝山大场淞沪抗战纪念坊

● Memorial Arch in commemoration of Song–Hu Battles in Dachang, Baoshan District in 1932

● 1937年宝山罗店激战处

● The site of a fierce battle in Luodian, Baoshan District in 1937

嘉定的风景

The scenery of Jiading

嘉定的风景

The scenery of Jiading

建于明代的嘉定秋霞圃

Qiuxia Garden in Jiading built in Ming Dynasty

建于宋代的嘉定孔庙

Confucian temple in Jiading built in Song Dynasty

- 建于明代的朱家角放生桥
- Life-Free Bridge in Zhujiajiao built in Ming Dynasty

- 青浦朱家角镇
- Zhujiajiao in Qingpu

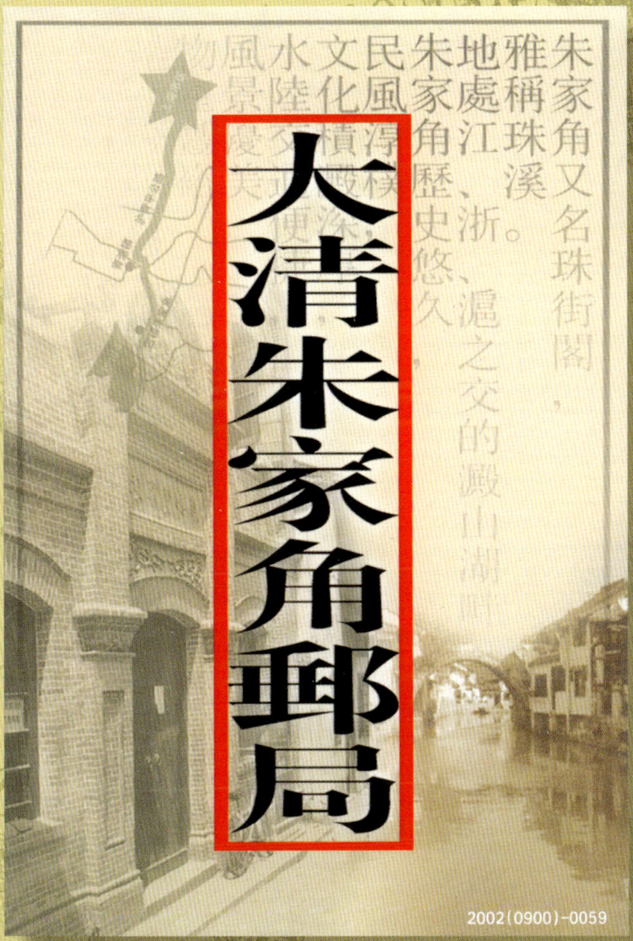

建于 1862 年的朱家角邮局

Zhujiajiao Post Office built in 1862

青浦博物馆

Qingpu Museum

建于唐代的青浦泖塔

Mao Pagoda in Qingpu built in Tang Dynasty

建于唐代的青浦青龙寺

Qinglong Temple in Qingpu built in Tang Dynasty

● 西气东输工程上海青浦末站

● The terminal of West—East National Gas Transmission Project in Qingpu, Shanghai

● 建设中的青浦

● Qingpu under construction

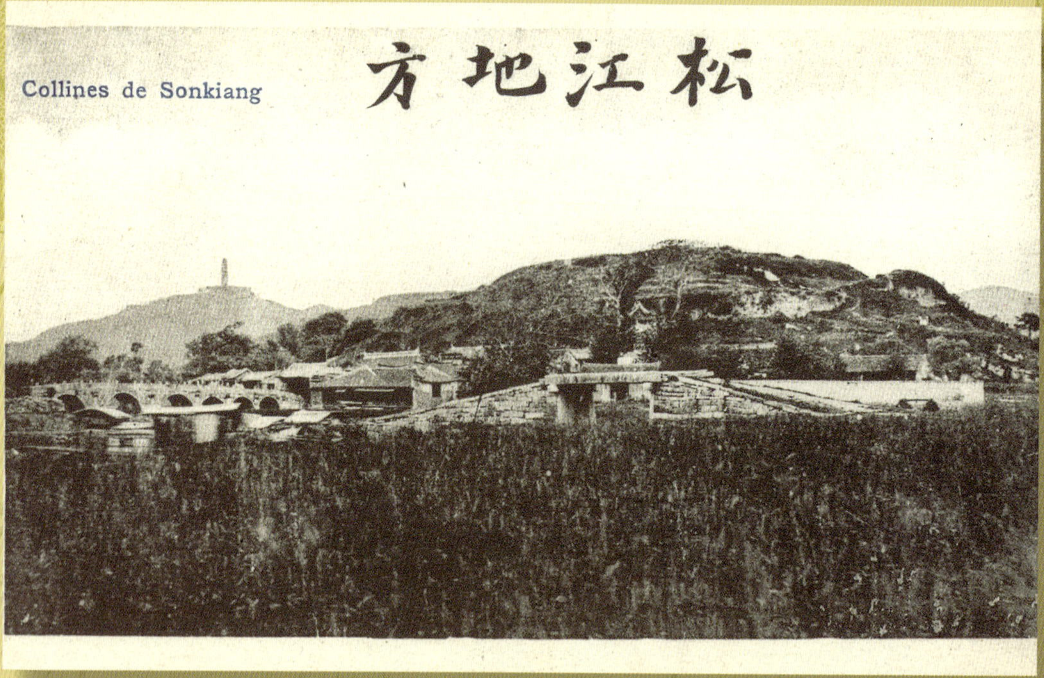

20 世纪初的松江佘山

She Shan in Songjiang in the 1900s

21 世纪初佘山国家旅游度假区

Sheshan State Forest Park in the 2000s

建于1899年的佘山天文台

She Shan Observatory built in 1899

改建于1935年的佘山天主教堂

Roman Catholic Cathedral in She Shan rebuilt in 1935

十

城乡风貌

Urban and Rural Scenery

● 建于宋代的松江方塔

● The square tower in Songjiang built in Song Dynasty

松江老城门

The City Gateway in Songjiang

建于元代的云间(松江的别名)第一楼

The First Building of Yunjian(another name for Songjiang) was built in Yuan Dynasty.

● 沿河而建的民宅

● Private residences built by the river

上海水乡

The region of rivers and lakes in Shanghai

十

城乡风貌

Urban and Rural Scenery

金山海滩

Beach in Jinshan

闵行七宝古镇

Qibao Ancient Town in Minhang District

乡村的民居

Folk houses in the village

乡村的民居

Folk houses in the village

十

城乡风貌 Urban and Rural Scenery

● 居民的生活

● Residents′ life

- 早期的居民住宅区
- The early residential areas

No. 114. Creek of Chinese City.

以船为家的生活

Living on the boat

86 Chinese Country near Shanghai

"滚地龙"及棚户区

Gundilong and shanty towns

- 贫民简屋
- Simple and crude houses of poor people

- 市民住宅
- Residences of the citizens

十

城乡风貌 Urban and Rural Scenery

● 石库门住宅
● Residences in Shikumen

● 石库门住宅
● Residences in Shikumen

石库门弄堂

Shikumen Lane

石库门弄堂

Shikumen Lane

20世纪50年代市民住宅

The residences of the citizens in the 1950s

20世纪50年代闵行市民住宅

The residences of the citizens in Minhang in the 1950s

20 世纪 60 年代工人新村

New village of the workers in the 1960s

1965 年改建的闸北番瓜弄工人新村

New village of the workers in Fanguanong, Zhabei rebuilt in 1965

20世纪90年代的公寓楼

Apartment blocks in the 1990s

20世纪90年代的农民新村

New village of the farmers in the 1990s

- 普陀中远两湾城
- Zhong Yuan Liang Wan Cheng in Putuo District

- 古北新村建设
- Gubei New Village was under construction

浦东的生活社区

Community Life in Pudong

浦东的生活社区

Community Life in Pudong

徐汇李鸿章故居

Former residence of Li Hongzhang in Xuhui District

徐汇蒋介石故居

Former residence of Chiang Kai-shek in Xuhui District

浦东黄炎培故居

Former residence of Huang Yanpei in Pudong

静安蔡元培故居

Former residence of Cai Yuanpei in Jing'an

青浦陈云故居

Former residence of Chen Yun in Qingpu District

浦东张闻天故居

Former residence of Zhang Wentian in Putong District

20世纪40年代高桥海塘工程建设

The construction of seawall project in Gaoqiao in the 1940s

高桥海塘

Seawall project in Gaoqiao

20世纪40年代污水处理工程建设

The construction of sewage disposal project in the 1940s

北新泾污水清炼厂水池

Sewage disposal project in Beixinjing

建于1896年的公大第一纱厂

The first Gongda cotton spinning mill built in 1896

进入棉纺织厂的工人

Workers of a cotton spinning mill were walking into the factory

公大一厂织机车间

The weaving room of Gongda cotton spinning mill

位于杨浦平凉路的公大一厂全景

The overall view of Gongda cotton spinning mill located on Pingliang Road in Yangpu District

1960年江南造船厂制造的万吨远洋轮"东风号"

The oceangoing ship called "Dong Feng" with a carrying capacity of 10 thousand was built in the South Shipyard in 1960

上海外高桥造船有限公司造船场景

The shipbuilding scene of Shanghai Waigaoqiao Shipbuilding Company

● 始建于1972年的上海石油化工总厂

● Shanghai Petroleum Chemical Engineering Corporation built in 1972

● 上海第一钢铁厂生产线

● The production lines of Shanghai First Steel works

宝山钢铁厂原料码头

Raw material wharf of Shanghai Baosteel Group Corporation

宝钢第一炉

The first heat of steel in Shanghai Baosteel Group Corporation

- 始建于1978年的上海宝山钢铁总厂
- Shanghai Baosteel Group Corporation built in 1978

- 1985年宝钢一期工程投产
- The first-stage construction of Baosteel Group Corporation was launched in 1985

十

城乡风貌

Urban and Rural Scenery

上海郊区农田

Suburban farmland in Shanghai

上海郊区农田

Suburban farmland in Shanghai

都市农业生产

Agricultural industry in the city

建于明代的浦东张家楼天主堂，为近代上海天主教的发祥地

Zhangjialou Catholic Church in Pudong District built in Ming Dynasty was the cradle land of Shanghai Catholic Church in modern times

Église de Tsang-ka-leu, P'outong.
浦東張家樓天主堂

建于明代的浦东钦赐仰殿，为上海道教正一派道观

Qinciyang Temple in Pudong District built in Ming Dynasty was the Daoist temple of Zhengyi sect in Shanghai

- 1990年开发开放浦东
- Pudong was opened up for development in 1990

● 浦东外高桥保税区

● Waigaoqiao Bonded Zone in Pudong

● 浦东外高桥保税区

● Waigaoqiao Bonded Zone in Pudong

浦东金桥出口加工区

Jiaoqiao Export Processing Zone in Pudong

浦东金桥出口加工区

Jiaoqiao Export Processing Zone in Pudong

浦东张江高科技园区

Zhangjiang Hi-tech Park in Pudong

浦东张江高科技园区

Zhangjiang Hi-tech Park in Pudong

● 浦东孙桥现代农业开发区

● Pudong Sunqiao Modern Agriculture Development Zone in Pudong, Shanghai

● 浦东陆家嘴金融贸易区

● Pudong Lujiazui Finance and Trade Zone

浦东新区行政中心和世纪广场

Administrative center and Century Square in Pudong New Area

浦东新区行政中心

Administrative center in Pudong New Area

日晷的夜景

The night scene of sundial

世纪广场的夜景

The night scene of Century Square

上海科技馆景观

The scene of Shanghai Technology Museum in the day

上海科技馆夜景

Shanghai Technology Museum at night

上海东方艺术中心景观

The scene of Shanghai Oriental Art Center in the day

上海东方艺术中心夜景

Shanghai Oriental Art Center at night

上海世纪公园

Shanghai Century Park

上海世纪公园

Shanghai Century Park

上海海洋水族馆

Shanghai Ocean Aquarium

上海海洋水族馆

Shanghai Ocean Aquarium

十

城乡风貌 Urban and Rural Scenery

上海东方电视台

Shanghai Oriental TV Station

浦东游泳馆

Pudong natatorium

浦东商业城

The commercial city in Pudong

浦东正大广场

Super Brand Plaza in Pudong

浦东陆家嘴景观

The scene of Lujiazui in Pudong District

2008年建成的上海环球金融中心(492米)

Shanghai World Financial Center was built in 2008 with a height of 492 meters

浦东游乐场

The pleasure ground in Pudong

浦东世纪大道

Pudong Century Avenue

摩天大楼——金茂大厦

Jin Mao Tower and the skyscrapers

浦东国际会议中心

International Convention Centre in Pudong

浦东的晨曦

The first sun rays in the morning in Pudong

浦东的晨曦

The first sun rays in the morning in Pudong

浦东的夜色

The night scene in Pudong

浦东的夜色

The night scene in Pudong

入夜的浦东流光溢彩

The brilliant night of Pudong

入夜的浦东流光溢彩

The brilliant night of Pudong

浦东陆家嘴远眺

A distant view of Lujiazui in Pudong

浦东陆家嘴金融贸易区新貌

The new look of Lujiazui Financial and Trade Zone in Pudong District

上海大学图书馆

Shanghai University Library

上海交通大学凯旋门

The triumphal arch of Shanghai Jiaotong University

松江大学城

Songjiang College Town

松江大学城体育馆

The indoor stadium of the Songjiang College Town

上海体育宫棒球场

The ball park of Shanghai Indoor Stadium

上海国际网球中心

Shanghai International Tennis Center

上海马术运动场

Shanghai Equestrian Field

上海自行车赛车场

Shanghai cycling stadium

十

城乡风貌 Urban and Rural Scenery

上海水上运动场

Shanghai Water Sports Center

上海国际高尔夫俱乐部

Shanghai International Golf Club

上海国际赛车场

Shanghai International Circuit

上海国际赛车场

Shanghai International Circuit

十 城乡风貌 Urban and Rural Scenery

闸北公园

Zhabei Park

黄兴公园

Huangxing Park

复兴公园秋天景色

The autumn scenery in Fuxing Park

复兴公园冬天景色

The winter scenery in Fuxing Park

大宁灵石公园

Da Ning Ling Shi Park

塘桥公园

Tangqiao Park

延中绿地公园

Yanzhong Green Land Park

宝山临江公园

Linjiang Park in Baoshan District

上海动物园

Shanghai Zoo

上海植物园

Shanghai Botanical Garden

东方绿舟青少年教育活动基地

Oriental Green Boat, the extracurricular activities base for juveniles

"热带风暴"水上乐园

Tropical Storm Water Park

十

城乡风貌 Urban and Rural Scenery

淀山湖风景区

The beauty spot of Dian Shan Lake

青浦大观园

Grand View Garden in Qingpu District

江湾湿地

Jiangwan Wetland

共青森林公园

Gongqing Forest Park

● 崇明东滩自然保护区

● Chongming Dongtan Reservation Area

● 崇明东滩自然保护区

● Chongming Dongtan Reservation Area

● 横沙岛——未来的生态休闲岛

● Hengsha Island — a special leisure island in the future

● 长兴岛将建成现代化船舶制造基地

● Changxing Island will be built into a modern ship-constructing base

20世纪70年代上海市区鸟瞰

A bird's–eye view of Shanghai in the 1970s

20世纪80年代上海市区鸟瞰

A bird's–eye view of Shanghai in the 1980s

不断升高的城市天际线

The nsing city skyline

20 世纪 90 年代上海市区鸟瞰

A bird's-eye view of Shanghai in the 1990s

21世纪初上海市区鸟瞰

A bird's-eye view of Shanghai in the 2000s

21世纪初上海市区鸟瞰

A bird's-eye view of Shanghai in the 2000s

- 夜上海鸟瞰
- A bird's–eye view of Shanghai at night

- 夜上海鸟瞰
- A bird's–eye view of Shanghai at night

上海城市新风貌

A new look of Shanghai

上海城市新风貌

A new look of Shanghai

Carte postale
union postale
LOCAL POST
人民邮政
明信片
上海外白渡桥
CARD.
中国
上海

图书在版编目（CIP）数据

美好城市的百年变迁：明信片上看上海／姚丽旋编著．—上海：上海大学出版社，2010.4
ISBN 978-7-81118-593-5

Ⅰ.①美…　Ⅱ.①姚…　Ⅲ.①名信片－中国－图集　②上海市－地方史－20世纪　Ⅳ.①G894.1　②K295.1

中国版本图书馆 CIP 数据核字（2010）第 036153 号

责任编辑：傅玉芳　柯国富
技术编辑：孟　玫
装帧设计：柯国富

美好城市的百年变迁——明信片上看上海

The Centennial Changes of the Dynamic City

Seeing Shanghai From the Postcards

姚丽旋　编著

Compiled by Yao Lixuan

上海大学出版社出版发行
（上海市上大路 99 号　邮政编码 200444）
（http://www.shangdapress.com 发行热线：021-66135110）
出版人：姚铁军

上海中华印刷有限公司印刷　各地新华书店经销
开本：889 × 1194　1/16　印张：45.5　字数：910 千
2010 年 4 月第 1 版　2010 年 4 月第 1 次印刷
ISBN 978-7-81118-593-5/G · 537
定价：320.00 元　上下册（精装）